Additional Praise

Fear Not, Creative dispels the rampant scaremongering that has gripped large portions of the creative industries. **CHRIS FRYAR**, *Grammy Award-winning drummer, Zac Brown Band*

Fear Not, Creative is a timely call for artists, designers, and makers that reminds us the most powerful creative force remains our humanity. Steven Potaczek offers a clear-eyed guide to navigating new tools while holding fast to [illegible] craft, and conviction. This book is both a challenge and an [illegible] the next era of creative work with imagination an[illegible] *Clinical Assistant Professor of Graphic Design,* [illegible] *Champaign, USA*

AI has people are scared, nervous, and wanting [illegible] in the sand. This book places human artists back in [illegible]rightful position: as the creative. **JASON TERRY**, *Assistant Professor of Music and Educational Innovation, Belmont University, USA*

Fear Not, Creative refuses both panic and hype of machine intelligence. Instead, it offers simultaneously lucid and meticulous accounts of what these technologies alter, and of what still resists them. In a moment saturated by synthetic and frictionless outputs, this book insists on the irreplicable nature and stubborn value of craft, vulnerability, and human residue. **JEFFREY HALSTEAD**, *Interdisciplinary Artist; Lecturer, School of Interior Design, Toronto Metropolitan University, Canada*

After more than 25 years of making records in a world that existed long before AI, I've learned that the work people remember is never the safest or most polished – it's the most human. Potaczek captures that truth beautifully, reminding us that in an age of infinite content, voice, authenticity, and creative courage, are what truly set meaningful work apart. **BRYAN WHITE**, *Grammy Award-winning country artist*

Most of the discourse about AI and the music industry falls into 1 of 2 categories: an enthusiastic but uncritical embrace, or a wholesale doom and gloom rejection. If the history of technology teaches us anything, it is that the way forward always lies in between and beyond these 2 extremes. In *Fear Not, Creative*, Potaczek pioneers the path forward with seasoned insight, clarity, and an engaging narrative style. **JASON LEE GUTHRIE**, *Associate Professor of Communication and Media Studies, Clayton State University, USA*

Packed with engaging questions and creative exercises, Potaczek has given us a timely and readable introduction to the unfolding field of creativity and AI. **ROBERT WILLEY**, *Associate Professor of Music, Ball State University, USA*

Fear Not, Creative is a timely and thought-provoking guide for artists navigating the rapid rise of artificial intelligence. Blending research, real-world examples, and practical reflection, Potaczek acknowledges the real disruptions AI is causing while confidently arguing that technology cannot replace the soul, vulnerability, and lived experience at the heart of true artistry. The book ultimately serves as both encouragement and strategy. **SHANE COLQUHOUN**, *Assistant Professor of Music Technology and Contemporary Music Styles, Alabama State University, USA*

Fear Not, Creative cuts through the anxiety surrounding artificial intelligence to offer artists a clearer view of what is actually changing amid the rise of AI, and what is not. Tracing the history of technological disruption while offering practical strategies for working alongside new tools, Potaczek argues that craft, authenticity, courage, and human connection are more valuable than ever. This timely book invites creatives to move beyond fear and build resilient, meaningful work in the age of AI. **BRYAN POWELL**, *Executive Director of the Association for Popular Music Education*

Fear Not, Creative

Futureproofing Artistic Work in the Age of AI

Steven Potaczek

Foreword by Jeff Goins

BLOOMSBURY ACADEMIC
NEW YORK • LONDON • OXFORD • NEW DELHI • SYDNEY

BLOOMSBURY ACADEMIC

Bloomsbury Publishing Inc, 1359 Broadway, 12th Floor, New York, NY 10018, USA
Bloomsbury Publishing Plc, 50 Bedford Square, London, WC1B 3DP, UK
Bloomsbury Publishing Ireland, 29 Earlsfort Terrace, Dublin 2, D02 AY28, Ireland

BLOOMSBURY, BLOOMSBURY ACADEMIC and the Diana logo are trademarks of Bloomsbury Publishing Plc

First published in the United States of America 2027

Cover design: Sally Rinehart
Cover image © Ryan McGinnis/Moment/Getty Images; iStock.com/aleksandarvelasevic; iStock.com/Remedios

A catalog record for this book is available from the Library of Congress.

ISBN: HB: 979-8-216-46091-6
PB: 979-8-216-46090-9
ePDF: 979-8-216-46092-3
ePub: 979-8-216-46093-0

Typeset by Deanta Global Publishing Services, Chennai, India
Printed and bound in the United States of America

For product safety related questions contact productsafety@bloomsbury.com.

To find out more about our authors and books visit www.bloomsbury.com and sign up for our newsletters.

Contents

Foreword

It's hard to be human these days.

Every day, I get an email or a text or see a social media post, all with the telltale signs of AI tampering. I can tell immediately if the piece was written by a human or not. When I ask the person, "Did you write this?" they usually fess up and say something like, "Of course I did! But AI helped me."

This, I think, will be the future of how we lie to each other.

"Yes, I picked out your birthday present! AI just helped a little."

"Of course I wrote every letter of that suspiciously perfect handwritten note. AI just helped a little bit."

I am, if you cannot tell, a little skeptical of this brave new world of artificial intelligence we are now entering. All the promises that have been touted—that we will have more free time to pursue the things that really matter to us, that we will be even more efficient and productive—are not proving to be true.

* * *

What I see, more and more, in this world that is increasingly dominated by technology is not humans rising to the challenge of thinking more deeply and solving more complex problems. What I see is more Amazon boxes sitting outside our homes, more meals delivered to our doorsteps, and more faces lit up by screens.

We are not necessarily "amusing ourselves to death" as Neil Postman once predicted. Rather, we are amusing ourselves out of really living.

And if that sounds like a little too much doom and gloom, well, I apologize. But it just seems obvious from where I'm standing. We are quickly losing grip on our humanity and only seem all too eager to give it up.

I, personally, do not fear the invasion of artificial intelligence into our lives. It does not seem to me to be a pernicious force in the world. What I am concerned about is what we as a species are giving up—namely, our ability to create.

The good news is we don't have to do this. As we watch a world reorient itself around what is easy and expeditious, we can reclaim what has been ours since the dawn of history, what we keep coming back to in our most dire times.

* * *

I probably don't have to tell you about the cave paintings our ancestors created centuries before we humans ever started writing things down. I don't have to show you the pictures of animals and monsters, the sculptures and tools our species has been creating for longer than we've had language. You know this story. You'ved lived it.

It is second nature for a child to create: to draw, to paint, to make up stories and tell them to friends and family. When I was a boy, probably around six or seven years old, I would run around my grandparents' front yard, pretending the stick in my hand was a sword, and fight imaginary dragons.

I was too shy to ask the neighbor to come and play with me, so I just did it where he would see me. The ruse looked like a charm and before long, he was out there with me, running around with me, participating in our shared adventure.

When we finished, he said to me, "You have quite an imagination."

I just looked at him, dumbfounded. That had never occurred to me. I just did what I knew, what seemed natural, and in a way, this is all I've been doing for most of my life: using whatever creative urges and skills I have to make something, hopefully in front of someone else, and invite them to join me in that act.

* * *

It's nothing revolutionary to say that we are all creative. We all know that by now. But are we all creating?

The ease of technology has filled our days with incessant task switching. Every moment of our day is filled with noise. We wake up, check in on the world via laptop or smartphone, get dressed, go to work, listen to a podcast, read the news, check email, answer some missed texts, grab lunch, check our phones, go back to work, check some more email, do a little "deep work" on whatever the current project is, go home, eat dinner, watch a show, and fall asleep.

Your life may not look exactly like the above, but it's probably not that far off. Most people in the modern world are living exactly this way. And there's nothing, *per se*, wrong with being productive. There's nothing even wrong with being busy in itself.

But what is all this busyness costing us? What, exactly, are we giving up to be so productive? And if we knew the bargain we were making, would we still make it?

I am reminded of an old story I once heard a preacher tell about a young monk speaking to his prior.

* * *

"Every day," the young monk says to his superior with a certain amount of pride, "I wake up at four o'clock and pray. Then I read the Psalms and go to mass. On my way to mass, I pray the rosary. After mass, I pray and sing three hymns . . ."

And on and on he goes with his whole day, just like that, filling in each looking crack of free time with some measure of obedience, a sacred practice or discipline he is hoping will win him the approval and adulation of the elder monk.

Instead, the prior looks at him aghast and says, "My dear boy! But when in the world do you have time to *think*?"

That is what we need more of now—time to think. To dream and wonder. To not make what the world demands of us to imagine another world altogether.

It is my view that only the artist can do this well. Only a creative soul can help us see what is not already available in the world. And in this new world, we would be wise to remember that.

This book is a reminder of who we are and what we could be. It's a nod to generations past and the power our predecessors had to not simply conform to the world but to help change it. Art does that, and art can do that again.

* * *

But there is a crucial element in all this that we cannot forget, and that is the human element. It is the matter of you and me and what we will do with this new world that may be coming for us whether we want it to or not.

We still have the power to make something new, to feel what it's like to be human and share our unique perspective. I have no doubt that AI will continue to improve at the technical aspects of creative output. But there is a difference between effective creativity and art that has a soul.

I'm sure you've seen and, more importantly, felt the difference: whether that's in a piece of music you adore, a film you keep rewatching, or a poem you once memorized. Art has the ability to remind us not just of who we are and where we come from but also what we could be. And the answer to that is always "more."

So, as Steven Potaczek reminds us, fear not. There is more opportunity here than threat, at least for those who are willing to look hard enough. We can and should accept the challenge of the age in which we now live, in the same way that medieval monks hid themselves away from the crises of their time to preserve literature from the ancient world, in the same way that Michelangelo and his peers elevated the art of one age and created another.

* * *

Our species is not unfamiliar to such challenges. Since the very beginning, we have been adapting to circumstances, pushing back against the pressures of every age, and finding a way to move beyond the noise and create. To make something new, something the world has never seen before. And I believe we, in some form or another, will continue doing so.

The question is, what will *you* do?

Jeff Goins, bestselling author of *Real Artists Don't Starve*

Part I

The Machine and the Mirror

Understanding How We Got Here

1 Is This the End of Creative Work?

You may not be interested in politics, but politics takes interest in you. The same applies to artificial intelligence many times over.[1]

OPENAI CO-FOUNDER AND COMPUTER SCIENTIST ILYA SUTSKEVER

A Massive Sea Change

I'll never forget working on my first album. I had been playing music since I was eight, but by junior year of high school the dream of writing and recording my *own* songs had taken over completely. In class, I probably appeared to be paying attention but, more often than not, I was working out lyrics in my head—much to the detriment of my grades, no doubt. After school, I'd pour myself into the piano, trying to marry melody and harmony to the words I'd imagined undercover. Every spare moment became a rehearsal for the life I wanted, chasing the possibility that one day I might be able to share my work with the world.

Pulling this off had financial implications, too. Working as a lifeguard at the community pool, I saved every penny to build a makeshift studio in my parents' basement. Microphones, instruments, cables, and the early digital recorders weren't cheap, and, though my folks were often happy to help, I knew that if I wanted to follow this dream most of the financing would fall to me.

Truth be told, I didn't even know what I was doing. I didn't know how to mic drums, layer guitars, or EQ a vocal. Nor did I know the first thing about editing, mixing, mastering, or distribution. Everything I learned came through trial, error, and a lot of late nights. There were no online tutorials, YouTube videos, or instructional manuals. It was grueling. I failed *a lot*. I felt so proud of that album though, because of the effort that went into it. I suppose it was the first semi-professional thing I could point to and say, "I made that." By the time the record hit store shelves, I had spent over *two years* crafting those eleven songs . . .

That was 1998. Looking back now though, it might as well as have been the Stone Age.

In May 2024, *Bloomberg* reported that Udio, one of the world's largest generative artificial intelligence (AI) music platforms, produces an average of ten fully formed songs a *second*.[2] That album I poured the entirety of my Junior and Senior years of high school into? AI now generates something similar in less than the time it's taking you to finish reading this sentence. Even for a tech geek like me, this explosive output is staggering. While impressive, this is a seismic shift that is already having significant ramifications for human creators.

We now live in a world where over one-fifth of new music uploaded to music streaming platforms is AI-generated.[3] Crowding playlists and saturating the market, that volume of material is also diverting precious revenue away from real, working musicians. Deezer, one of the world's top streaming services, predicts that by 2028 up to a quarter of artists' streaming income—which let me tell you, wasn't that wonderful to begin with—could be at risk.

We're seeing a similar pattern in other creative fields. In 2022, generative AI reached a point where the public could produce surprisingly realistic-looking images through simple text prompts. Within their first eighteen months, websites like Midjourney, DALL-E, and Stable Diffusion had generated over 15 billion photos. That's a *fifteen* with *nine* zeros attached. You know how long it took humanity to take that many pictures? 149 years.[4] What's a professional photographer or graphic designer to do when AI can output images thousands of times faster and cheaper? And all without the need to learn photography, lighting, or editing.

Text-to-image generators have also quickly risen to provide immediate home design ideas and inspiration to prospective architectural and interior design clients. The AI-powered website, Qbiq, claims that with its built-in suite of tools, "anyone can plan, visualize, and optimize any space in minutes."[5]

Another website, Laiout, promises to deliver "automated floor plans in seconds."[6] In response to tools like these, the popular architectural and interior design magazine *Dezeen* published an article in 2023 where its author warned that "there are signs that AI is becoming not only good, but terrifyingly good, to the point that it is . . . putting our jobs as architects unquestionably at risk."[7]

Generative AI is also rapidly infiltrating journalism. A 2024 systematic review by researchers Sonny, Hafied, Irwanto, and Latuheru revealed that:

- 73 percent of news organizations are using generative AI for writing automation,
- 68 percent of them are using it for data analysis, and
- 62 percent are using it for content personalization.[8]

That same year, a Pew Research Center poll found that a majority of Americans expect AI to significantly reduce journalism jobs within the next twenty years.[9]

Authors, illustrators, and book translators are feeling the same pressure. According to a 2024 survey by the Society of Authors, 26 percent of these individuals had already lost work due to generative AI, and 37 percent had lost income.[10] This isn't just a problem for major publishing companies or household names like Stephen King or David Baldacci. The latter actually spoke candidly at a 2025 Senate Subcommittee where he warned that the rise of generative tools is making publishers increasingly risk-averse, explaining: "That will mean lower profits for publishers, and less money to spend on new, emerging writers."[11] All this comes at a time when earnings were already declining, with most authors' median writing-related income hovering just over $20,000 according to a 2025 survey.[12]

Meanwhile, in Hollywood, Scarlett Johansson made headlines after discovering that the voice of OpenAI's *Sky* model bore an uncanny resemblance to her own. The revelation was especially unsettling given that Johansson claims OpenAI had previously approached her to voice the assistant—a request she declined.[13] While she is advocating for legislation to curb the technology, she lamented that she feels on her own, without much public support. If a globally recognized celebrity—with vast resources and legal teams at their disposal—feels vulnerable in this new world, imagine the position of everyday creatives whose names don't make headlines.

Take, for instance, the $4.04 billion global industry of voice actors, interpreters, and sound engineers whose work is now under threat. In France alone, approximately 12,500 professionals are employed in the localization of Hollywood films and television—translating, adapting, and voicing content for French-speaking audiences. Many of them are urgently calling on the government to grant legal protections. Patrick Kuban, an organizer with the French dubbing union Voix Off, warned: "If we don't have protection, all kinds of jobs will be lost: after the movie industry, it will be the media industry, the music industry, all the cultural industries."[14] The story echoes in Australia, where the Australian Association of Voice Actors warned a parliamentary committee that some 5,000 local voice actors are in danger of losing their work in radio and audiobook narration due to the perceived cost-cutting allure of AI-generated alternatives.[15]

Not even computer programmers are safe. In 2025, Meta CEO Mark Zuckerberg began tasking his expert team of coders with the responsibility to develop their in-house AI enough so it can perform the coding for future iterations of its suite of apps.[16] In essence, software engineers are being asked to feed a beast that is already eyeing them for its next meal. While the irony here is astounding, recent marketplace data does in fact reveal that there are fewer programmers in the United States than at any point since 1980.[17] Correlation may not necessarily imply causation, but you can't tell me Zuckerberg's coders aren't feeling a bit . . . uneasy.

The fact is that alarm bells are ringing from every corner of the labor economy. A recent poll of over 5,000 US adults showed that 64 percent believe that AI will lead to fewer jobs over the next twenty years.[18] Another study, given to over 48,000 people from forty-seven different countries revealed that "there is a striking increase in the number of people feeling worried about AI systems, rising from almost half (49%) of respondents in 2022 to 62% in 2024."[19] Even leading labor economists have yet to outline a clear roadmap for navigating the disruption AI may bring. While websites like Will Robots Take My Job? are attempting to provide answers, the reality is that no one truly knows how this technology will reshape the job market in *any* sector. And we haven't even gotten to the murky question of how tech companies are sourcing the data that trains these AIs to paint, code, design, compose, and write.

Everything You Make Now Belongs to AI

In 2025, *The Washington Post* analyzed Google's C4 dataset—the foundation for many leading AI models—and uncovered a troubling blend of proprietary, personal, and copyrighted content. Half of the top ten sources were major news outlets, including *The New York Times*, *Los Angeles Times*, *The Guardian*, *Forbes*, and *HuffPost*. None of these organizations were asked for permission, offered compensation, or even informed. More disturbingly, *The Washington Post* noted that most generative AI companies "do not document the contents of their training data—even internally—for fear of finding personal information about identifiable individuals, copyrighted material, and other data grabbed without consent."[20]

As of this writing, AI developers are under no legal obligation to reveal where their training data comes from. Their defense is that transparency would expose trade secrets. Even if the day comes where they're forced to answer for their practices, proving infringement on specific works may be next to impossible because these systems are so massive and intentionally opaque.

The result is a widespread fear among artists, writers, designers, software developers, and other knowledge workers that their life's work may be quietly ingested into a system that reproduces their style, replaces their role, and offers no compensation or credit in return. Composers worry that their songs are being used to train AI tools capable of churning out countless imitation tracks. Journalists fear that their investigative reporting is teaching bots how to summarize news faster. Designers are concerned that their portfolios are fueling image generators that offer clients cheaper, AI-made alternatives.

In response to mounting criticism from the creative sector, venture capital firms and tech company CEOs have increasingly lobbied for deregulation. For example, Udio's venture capitalist (VC) firm, Andreessen Horowitz, submitted to the U.S. Copyright Office that "imposing the cost of actual or potential copyright liability on the creators of AI models will either kill or significantly hamper their development."[21] In a lawsuit brought about by all of the major record labels against both Suno AI and Udio, the defendants argued that their use of the material falls within "fair use" exemptions of existing copyright law and subsequently accused the recording companies of pursuing legal action in an effort to "prevent competition."[22] While both companies have since settled with a few of the record labels, the cavalier attitude and dismissive stance of these companies toward rights holders demonstrates the pervasive attitude of Silicon Valley: *we can do whatever we want*. As more lawsuits like this begin to flood the court systems, tech company CEOs will undoubtedly be lobbying even more in response.

In a 2025 Senate hearing, OpenAI CEO Sam Altman warned that requiring content licensing to release powerful AI software would be "disastrous" for the United States' leadership in the field. This was a striking reversal from his testimony two years earlier, when he listed the creation of a new federal agency to license AI models as his "number one" recommendation for ensuring their safety.[23] The argument is basically that protecting creators' rights stands in sharp opposition to national security and financial incentive and therefore must be curtailed in pursuit of a greater good.

Governmental oversight swings violently on this issue. On one hand, several lawmakers—from both sides of the aisle—are holding subcommittee hearings to elevate the concerns of artists, authors, and creatives who fear their livelihoods are being eroded by unchecked development. Encouragingly, the European Union has taken a leadership role, signing international agreements pledging to support "safe, secure, and trustworthy" AI, and crafting legislation that enforces transparency and accountability.[24] By contrast, other policymakers are pushing for fewer restrictions, framing regulation as a threat to innovation rather than a safeguard for creatives and knowledge workers.

At an international 2025 AI summit in Paris, US Vice President JD Vance claimed that "AI future will not be won by handwringing about safety."[25] In short: less regulation, more opportunity. At its core, this perspective represents the viewpoint that AI safety needs to take a backseat to AI opportunity. "To restrict [AI's] development now," Vance said, "will not only unfairly benefit incumbents in the space, but it would also mean paralyzing one of the most promising technologies we've seen in generations."[26]

All this comes at a time when the general public is increasingly expressing deep concern about AI. A 2024 survey done by the Pew Research Center revealed that 51 percent of the respondents felt more concerned than excited about the increased use of AI, while only 11 percent expressed more excitement than concern.[27] This represents a significant shift from the same study performed in 2022, where just 38 percent reported more concern than excitement. In a 2025 Quinnipiac poll, Dr. Chetan Jaiswal, Associate Professor of Computer Science at Quinnipiac University, summarized these sentiments this way:

> There's growing frustration with companies that keep their AI practices behind closed doors, and widespread doubt that government is stepping up to regulate the technology. The message from the public is unmistakable: the transparency isn't there. Without it, confidence in both business and government erodes fast in an AI-driven world.[28]

One thing is certain: we cannot rely on the "better angels" of venture capitalists, tech companies, and government bureaucrats to protect creatives and our intellectual property.

So . . . Is Creative Work Doomed?

All this makes for a pretty bleak opening for a book that's titled *Fear Not, Creative*. I'm not going to sugarcoat anything here: countless artists feel ripped off by big tech, some have already lost their jobs, and the creative marketplace is quickly becoming more saturated than a sponge in a monsoon. To quote an article from the American Association for the Advancement of Science: "AI-based image generators have raised the prospect of the emergence not just of a radically new art movement but of the end of art itself—and especially of the artist as individual human genius."[29] That's pretty damning words for anyone who wields a paintbrush, pencil, computer, camera, or guitar for a living.

Let me not mince words: things are never going to be the same ever again. Change is imminent. And while the impact of generative AI may unfold unevenly over the coming years, it's all but certain to have a transformative effect on society, commerce, culture, and the creative professions. We can bury our heads in the sand and wish it away, but such dragons do not go so quietly into the night.

Instead, what I'm offering in the pages ahead is not false comfort, but a blueprint. A battle plan. A way to move forward with clarity, resilience, and purpose. Not just to weather the storm, but to build something stronger in its midst. Even as venture capitalists, politicians, tech CEOs, and media evangelists proclaim that AI will soon outperform the most brilliant among us, I'm telling you this: There *is* a future for your creative work. Even more audaciously, I believe we may be standing at the threshold of a creative renaissance—one in which artistic excellence, human insight, and imaginative daring will not only survive, but thrive. Perhaps even more than it has in a long time.

That future, however, will not belong to those who remain frozen in fear or passive in outrage. It will belong to those who choose to *engage*, to *evolve*, and to *own* their voice and craft more deeply than ever before. The creative professionals who rise in this new era will be those who recognize that while technology may change the tools and terrain, it cannot replace what is fundamentally human. It cannot originate soul, cannot risk vulnerability, and cannot own the stories it only observes.

This doesn't mean we need to reject all AI outright. Such a myopic view would be just as blind as pretending AI isn't having an impact on the world. No, we cannot refuse to evolve. But it is absolutely imperative that we take a step back and examine how we got here, what these tools can and cannot do, and how we *choose* to move forward—whether that means wholeheartedly embracing them, intentionally rejecting them, or taking a hybrid approach. Answering questions like these will be a deeply personal choice, as they will undoubtedly influence your creative values, voice, opportunities, threats, and unique selling proposition in the marketplace.

This book is here to help you explore those choices—not by giving you a prescription, but by offering perspective, encouragement, and provocation. Each chapter is designed to unpack a key theme in the larger story of art, craft, and commerce in the age of AI. You'll find personal stories, hard questions, industry insights, and practical exercises, all aimed at helping you define what it means to create in a time of cultural transformation.

As you'll come to see, the challenge we face isn't altogether new. If we zoom out far enough, history tells a familiar tale. It's worth noting that creativity always endures. Not because culture and technology remained the same, but because the impulse to communicate, to express, and to move others was simply too powerful to extinguish. Every era of disruption gives rise to new forms. Every collapse opens space for innovation. Take heart: this is not the end of human art, but it may well be the birth of a new season.

Don't mistake my optimism for naivety. None of this will be easy. But in many ways, this is how it has always been for creatives. No one in their right mind has ever thought that a career in the arts might be an easy way to get rich quick. We creatives know that we do this because we have what my friend, music producer Monroe Jones, calls "the sickness." We do it because, deep down, we have a low-grade fever that *compels* us to create. We do it because the idea of doing anything else fills us with more dread than facing the risk of actually going for it. I see you, fellow creative, and I walk beside you.

Here's the truth that the Silicon Valley cheerleaders never admit: AI is not magic. It's math. It's fast and at times, even impressive. But it's still math. It doesn't create; it can only recombine, remix, and regurgitate. It's a mimic without meaning. Yes, it can generate, but it cannot genuinely *make*. Only humanity can do that.

And that's the difference. That's the reason I'm writing to you. Not to convince you that everything is going to be fine and easy, but to remind you that the creative spirit has always burned brightest when the world seemed darkest. With a perspective rooted in history, insight drawn from today's marketplace, and a clear-eyed view of what it means to be human, I believe artists can not only navigate this moment, but can help shape it.

This book is an invitation to stop waiting for clarity to descend and to start building the future you want to see. Not with ignorant fear or pining nostalgia, but with boldness, grit, and the unshakable belief that the world still needs *your* voice. This is a field manual for artists, designers, makers, and dreamers who refuse to disappear into the noise. It's a defense of craft in an age of instant content. It's not about wishing for an era gone by, but a challenge to those of us who believe in the power of originality, even when it feels like the whole world has traded its soul for novelty without substance. Whether you're a video game designer, author, composer, illustrator, or any kind of maker who breathes life into ideas, there is a way forward for you. And I want to help you find it.

The Roadmap

I don't know where you are on your creative journey. Maybe you're just starting out, hoping there's still a place in the world for what you dream of making. Maybe you're a working professional, feeling the pressure of a shifting marketplace and uncertain what it means for your livelihood. Or maybe you're a passionate hobbyist, simply trying to make sense of how AI works and what all this means for the future of creativity. Wherever you find yourself, know that you are welcome. My aim in writing this book is to provide you with clarity, empowerment, and a strategy to flourish. Not with sweeping generalities, but with specific, grounded steps, insight into both the tech industry and the creative economy, and real tools to help you navigate this pivotal moment.

In the chapters ahead, we'll unpack specifically what AI is . . . and what it isn't. We'll cut through the hype, the fearmongering, and the corporate spin to understand how we got here and where things are headed. You won't need a background in computer science; this is a plainspoken guide written specifically for creatives who want to get back to making, not deciphering tech jargon.

We'll break down the buzzwords: "agents," "reasoning models," "neural networks"—anthropomorphic terms that make AI seem human when it is anything but. We'll explore what these technologies actually do, how they're trained, and how they've begun encroaching on creative fields once considered distinctively human. At the same time, we'll interrogate the assumptions that underlie the AI gold rush and the unsustainable promises being made by Silicon Valley. For all the vapid declarations about machines replacing us, many rely on narratives that simply aren't true.

With an eye to the future, we'll also look at the history of art and commerce. We'll explore the vulnerabilities of our current moment as well the opportunities for tomorrow. We'll examine actual research grounded in scientific fact, not hype based on the need to raise money or political influence. And we'll take an honest look at ourselves and where we, as a collective creative community, may have to take some of the blame for how generative AI has been able to scrape and copy our work so easily.

More importantly, we'll explore what makes you, as a human artist, irreplaceable. We'll rethink what value means in today's creative economy, how to stand out in the marketplace, and how to build an audience that loves what you—and only you—can do. We'll discuss how to build trust with an audience that sees your work as more than a commodity, and as connection. And we'll talk strategy: how to futureproof your career, sharpen your craft, and develop a resilient, confident creative practice in a world that is constantly in flux.

The book is broken up into two parts: "The Machine and the Mirror: Understanding How We Got Here" and "Reclaiming Creative Power: How We Move Forward." While you're free to skip ahead to whatever chapter sparks your curiosity, I encourage you to take the journey in order. Everything is deliberately structured so each chapter builds on the last, rising toward the next.

Perhaps even more important than what I've written are the intentional moments of reflection that are built-in. This book isn't meant to be read passively like the never-ending social media posts we scroll past on our phones. It's meant to engage and meet you in the tension between your creative calling and the uncertainty you may be feeling.

At the end of each chapter, you'll find a set of reflection questions and creative exercises. The questions are there to help you pause, digest, and listen—not to me, but to yourself. They're here to help you explore what's stirring inside and how you're making sense of it. Respond in a way that feels most true to you.

The exercises, meanwhile, are designed to bring you back to doing. Whether you're an architect, designer, or tattoo artist, these practices are simple, tangible ways to reconnect with the muscle memory of creating. Some will stretch you. Others might feel silly. But each one is meant to help you reinhabit your role as an artist. Try to do at least one of them each chapter.

Don't think of these as homework, but more like handrails: steadying practices that help anchor you as everything around you shifts. In an age that's always accelerating, these pauses can be be profound moments of slowing down, contemplating, and moving forward with clarity, confidence, and creative autonomy. As tempting as it might be to skip these sections, I encourage you to take the time to wrestle with them. Allocate the space needed to define your thoughts and beliefs through intentional contemplation and creative exploration.

Finally, if you have an artistic community around you, it may be beneficial to go through this book with them. Some of what's ahead may challenge you, and having people to process it with can spark helpful conversations. In my experience, hearing how others wrestle with the same questions often reveals answers I didn't know I was looking for. While it might feel awkward to invite a friend or two into a book study with you, I'd encourage you to consider it anyways and make this a journey you take together with others.

Your Turn

As the opening chapter, this is where you can develop a practice that carries through the entire book. While you don't need to make every answer a manifesto or every exercise a masterpiece, let this be a space where you refine your voice, clarify your values, and shape a creative identity that no machine could replicate.

So, before you move onto the next chapter, take a few minutes to reflect, create, wrestle, or even push back. Consider it an investment in your future self.

Questions

1 Imagine reaching the last page of this book. What do you want to feel then? What worries do you hope will no longer weigh you down?

2 What do you think will differentiate human artists from AI in the coming years? What uniquely human qualities are irreplaceable?

3 How do you define your own creative voice? Can you articulate what makes it distinctly human?

Exercises

1 Timeline of Change:
Sketch out a timeline of your creative journey, noting moments when a new technology impacted your work either positively or negatively. How did those events help shape who you are as an artist today?

2 Three-Column Audit:
Create a three-column list with these headers: "AI Can Help Me With," "AI Should Be Avoided For," and "AI Can't Replace." Fill in each based on your current creative process. It's okay if these change in the coming chapters; just consider how you feel about things in this moment.

3 I Made That:
At the start of the chapter, I shared how proud I was of my first album because it was the first semi-professional thing I could point to and say, "I made that." What was the first creative piece you made that truly felt like *yours*? The kind of thing that made you think, "This really reflects who I am," or "Maybe this is what I'm meant to do with my life."
If you still have access to it, pull it out (if not, reconstruct it in your mind). As you listen to, look at, or hold it, write a simple journal entry that reflects:

- How did this work shift my sense of identity or purpose?
- What made it feel uniquely *me*?
- What value did it offer to others?

Notes

1 Sutskever, Ilya. "Ilya Sutskever, U of T Honorary Degree Recipient, June 6, 2025." *University of Toronto*, June 6, 2025. Accessed December 8, 2025. https://www.youtube.com/watch?v=zuZ2zaotrJs.

2 Metz, Rachel. "The AI Music Era Is Here. Not Everyone Is a Fan." *Bloomberg*, May 6, 2024. Accessed December 9, 2025. https://www.bloomberg.com/news/articles/2024-05-06/suno-udio-and-more-the-ai-music-era-is-here-not-everyone-is-a-fan.

3 Koetsier, John. "20,000 AI-Generated Songs Uploaded to Deezer Every Single Day." *Forbes*, April 16, 2025. Accessed December 9, 2025. https://www.forbes.com/sites/johnkoetsier/2025/04/16/20000-ai-generated-songs-uploaded-to-deezer-every-single-day/.

4 Hobbs, Amy. "[Stats] How Many Photos Have Ever Been Taken?" *Fstoppers*, March 10, 2012. Accessed December 9, 2025. https://fstoppers.com/other/stats-how-many-photos-have-ever-been-taken-5173.

5 Qbiq. Accessed December 9, 2025. https://www.qbiq.ai/.

6 Laiout. Accessed December 9, 2025. https://www.laiout.co/.

7 Leach, Neil. "AI is Putting Our Jobs as Architects Unquestionably at Risk." *Dezeen*, February 13, 2023. Accessed December 9, 2025. https://www.dezeen.com/2023/02/13/ai-architecture-jobs-risk-neil-leach-opinion/.

8 Sonni, Alem Febri, Hafied, Hasdiyanto, Irwanto, Irwanto, and Latuheru, Rido. 2024. "Digital Newsroom Transformation: A Systematic Review of the Impact of Artificial Intelligence on Journalistic Practices, News Narratives, and Ethical Challenges." *Journalism and Media* 5, no. 4: 1554–1570. https://doi.org/10.3390/journalmedia5040097.

9 Lipka, Michael. "Americans Largely Foresee AI Having Negative Effects on News, Journalists." *Pew Research Center*, April 28, 2025. Accessed December 9, 2025. https://www.pewresearch.org/short-reads/2025/04/28/americans-largely-foresee-ai-having-negative-effects-on-news-journalists/.

10 SoA Policy Team. "SoA Survey Reveals a Third of Translators and Quarter of Illustrators Losing Work to AI." *Society of Authors*, April 11, 2024. Accessed December 9, 2025. https://societyofauthors.org/2024/04/11/soa-survey-reveals-a-third-of-translators-and-quarter-of-illustrators-losing-work-to-ai/.

11 The Authors Guild. "Authors Guild Member David Baldacci Testifies Before Senate Crime Subcommittee on AI Theft." *The Authors Guild*, July 16, 2025. Accessed December 9, 2025. https://authorsguild.org/news/david-baldacci-senate-testimony-ai-theft.

12 The Authors Guild. "Key Takeaways from 2023 Author Income Survey." *The Authors Guild*, October 25, 2023. Accessed December 9, 2025. https://authorsguild.org/news/key-takeaways-from-2023-author-income-survey/.

13 David, Emilia. "Lawyers Say OpenAI Could Be in Real Trouble with Scarlett Johansson." *The Verge*, May 22, 2024. Accessed December 9, 2025. https://www.theverge.com/2024/5/22/24162429/scarlett-johansson-openai-legal-right-to-publicity-likeness-midler-lawyers.

14 Russell, Emma. "'You're Stealing My Identity!': The Movie Voiceover Artists Going to War with AI." *The Guardian*, July 3, 2025. Accessed December 9, 2025. https://www.theguardian.com/film/2025/jul/03/ai-foreign-language-voiceover-artists.

15 Ibid.

16 Marks, Gene. "Business Tech News: Zuckerberg Says AI Will Replace Mid-Level Engineers Soon." *Forbes*, January 26, 2025. Accessed December 9, 2025. https://www.forbes.com/sites/quickerbettertech/2025/01/26/business-tech-news-zuckerberg-says-ai-will-replace-mid-level-engineers-soon/.

17 Van Dam, Andrew. "More Than a Quarter of Computer-Programming Jobs Just Vanished. What Happened?" *The Washington Post*, March 14, 2025. Accessed December 9, 2025. https://www.washingtonpost.com/business/2025/03/14/programming-jobs-lost-artificial-intelligence/.

18 McClain, Colleen, Kennedy, Brian, Gottfried, Jeffrey, Anderson, Monica, and Pasquini, Giancarlo. "How the U.S. Public and AI Experts View Artificial Intelligence." *Pew Research Center*, April 3, 2025. Accessed December 9, 2025. https://www.pewresearch.org/2025/04/03/us-public-and-ai-experts-methodology/.

19 Gillespie, N., Lockey, S., Ward, T., Macdade, A., and Hassed, G. "Trust, Attitudes and Use of Artificial Intelligence: A Global Study 2025." The University of Melbourne and KPMG, 2025. https://doi.org/10.26188/28822919.

20 Schaul, Kevin, Chen, Szu Yu, and Tiku, Nitasha. "Inside the Secret List of Websites That Make AI Like ChatGPT Sound Smart." *The Washington Post*,

April 19, 2023. Accessed December 9, 2025. https://www.washingtonpost.com/technology/interactive/2023/ai-chatbot-learning/.

21 Tencer, Daniel. "Andreessen Horowitz's Thoughts on AI Show What the Music Industry Is Up Against in 2024." *Music Business Worldwide*, January 3, 2024. Accessed December 9, 2025. https://www.musicbusinessworldwide.com/andreessen-horowitzs-thoughts-on-ai-shows-what-the-music-Industry-is-up-against in 2024/.

22 Tencer, Daniel. "As Suno and Udio Admit Training AI with Unlicensed Music, Record Industry Says: 'There's Nothing Fair About Stealing an Artist's Life's Work.'" *Music Business Worldwide*, August 5, 2024. Accessed December 9, 2025. https://www.musicbusinessworldwide.com/as-suno-and-udio-admit-training-ai-with-unlicensed-music-record-industry-says-theres-nothing-fair-about-stealing-an-artists-lifes-work/.

23 De Vynck, Gerrit and Tiku, Nitasha. "AI Execs Used to Beg for Regulation. Not Anymore." *The Washington Post*, May 8, 2025. Accessed December 9, 2025. https://www.washingtonpost.com/technology/2025/05/08/altman-congress-openai-regulation/.

24 European Union. "Regulation (EU) 2024/1689 of the European Parliament and of the Council of 13 June 2024 Laying Down Harmonised Rules on Artificial Intelligence and Amending Regulations (EC) No 300/2008, (EU) No 167/2013, (EU) No 168/2013, (EU) 2018/858, (EU) 2018/1139 and (EU) 2019/2144 and Directives 2014/90/EU, (EU) 2016/797 and (EU) 2020/1828 (Artificial Intelligence Act)." *Official Journal of the European Union* L 1689, July 12, 2024. https://eur-lex.europa.eu/eli/reg/2024/1689/oj/eng.

25 Kaput, Mike. "JD Vance's AI Speech in Europe: 'AI Future Will Not Be Won By Hand-Wringing About Safety.'" *Marketing Artificial Intelligence Institute*, February 18, 2025. Accessed December 9, 2025. https://www.marketingaiinstitute.com/blog/jd-vance-ai-speech.

26 Ibid.

27 McClain, Colleen, Kennedy, Brian, Gottfried, Jeffrey, Anderson, Monica, and Pasquini, Giancarlo. "How the U.S. Public and AI Experts View Artificial Intelligence." *Pew Research Center*, April 3, 2025. Accessed December 9, 2025. https://www.pewresearch.org/internet/2025/04/03/views-of-risks-opportunities-and-regulation-of-ai/.

28 Quinnipiac University. "The Age of Artificial Intelligence: Americans Wary of Impact on Daily Life, See Harm to Education, Benefits to Medical Advances, Quinnipiac University National Poll Finds; Americans Expect AI Will Cause Job Losses But Workers Don't Think Their Own Jobs Will Disappear." April 16, 2025. Accessed December 9, 2025. https://poll.qu.edu/poll-release?releaseid=3923.

29 Zylinska, Joanna. "Art in the Age of Artificial Intelligence." *Science* 380, no. 6650 (2023): 1110–1112. https://doi.org/10.1126/science.adh0575.

2 A Brief History of AI—Through a Creative Lens

To be ignorant of what occurred before you were born is to remain always a child.[1]

CICERO

It started as a joke. A simple program, written to mock the idea of machine "intelligence," was supposed to end the debate once and for all. ELIZA couldn't think. It couldn't feel. It could only rearrange words—a parlor trick dressed up as conversation. But in 1966, that was enough to leave audiences awestruck. Many even wondered if the program might be sentient. The irony was brutal: in trying to dismantle the illusion of machine intelligence, ELIZA's creator, Professor Joseph Weizenbaum, had made it stronger.

Technologically, ELIZA was primitive. It could do little more than pluck a keyword from your sentence and toss back a question. A clever trick, nothing more. Yet even after Weizenbaum explained the mechanics in painstaking detail, people clung to the fantasy. His own secretary asked if she could be alone with it, convinced the machine was listening to her.[2]

The tendency for humans to project consciousness onto machines has since become known as the *ELIZA effect*, our psychological susceptibility to over-attribute understanding or awareness to computers, especially when they use language. As AI has grown more fluent and lifelike, this effect has only gotten stronger. Today, roughly one in five Americans believe AI is sentient, and about one in three believe that *AGIs* (artificial general intelligences)—systems capable of outperforming performing humans across multiple domains—already exist.[3] But just like Weizenbaum's ELIZA back in the 1960s, today's AI is not alive. It doesn't think, feel, or have any personal beliefs. It can't even grasp what those concepts mean.

Tools like ChatGPT are designed to simulate human dialogue as a means of providing a simplified interface. Upon being asked, the algorithm itself will explain this anthropomorphic style is a communication choice, not a reflection of consciousness:

> I don't actually have thoughts, feeling, or experiences. When I sound conversational, empathetic, or introspective, I'm simulating those tones based on patterns in human language. I generate responses by predicting the most likely next words based on your input and my training data—not from any inner experience or awareness. So if I say something that sounds like I'm reflecting, caring, or thinking independently, it's really just a reflection of how people tend to speak in similar contexts. There's no "me" behind the curtain—just computation.[4]

Like ELIZA, modern chatbot programs rely on clever programming techniques that certainly deserve some of the accolades they've been awarded. But to ascribe any level of humanity to them is fundamentally erroneous. Everything AI generates is based on mathematical probabilities of what words or ideas are most likely to come next, given the input we provide. I'll explain more about this shortly, but for now you might think of AI as a superpowered autocomplete.

While this book isn't intended to get bogged down in the technical weeds of artificial intelligence, I do believe it's essential to provide a basic framework that's both accessible and relevant to creatives. In this chapter, I'll walk you through a brief historical overview of key turning points in AI's development, followed by a plainspoken explanation of how many of today's systems actually work. By zooming out to take this bird's eye view, we'll gain a clearer sense of what's really happening under the hood. More importantly, we'll start to unpack where AI tends to excel, and where it inevitably falls short. Let's dive in.

Not the First Rodeo

Unless you've been living in an off-the-grid cabin for the past thirty years, you've undoubtedly been using AI for quite some time. Every time you've opened Microsoft Word or Google Docs and the program autocorrected *teh* to *the*, that's AI. When you ask "Siri" or "Alexa" to play your favorite song? Same.

When your camera automatically adjusted the focus of the lens to sharpen on the face of the person in-frame? AI. And when your credit card company calls to ask if you just made a purchase in Cancun, it's because an AI model detected something unusual in your spending patterns. AI isn't something new; it's been woven in the fabric of everyday life for decades.

The term "artificial intelligence" actually dates all the way back to 1955, when Dartmouth College Professor John McCarthy coined the phrase. A computer scientist, McCarthy was fascinated with the idea of machine learning and wanted to establish the field as a legitimate academic discipline. Along with fellow computing pioneers Marvin Minsky, Nathaniel Rochester, and Claude Shannon, McCarthy drafted a proposal for what would become the "Dartmouth Summer Research Project on Artificial Intelligence": a two-month, ten-person study that would officially mark AI as a field of academic study.

In the decades that followed, researchers focused largely on what became known as "symbolic AI," where intelligence was modeled through logic and rule-based systems.[5] ELIZA was one of these early systems, soon to be followed by other primitive AI programs. The general public was fascinated by this emerging technology, which was beginning to find its way into pop culture. When *Star Trek* first appeared in 1966, audiences were introduced to the ship's computer—a helpful system that communicated with a calm, female voice that almost seemed alive. Just a few years later, Stanley Kubrick's *2001: A Space Odyssey* introduced the world to HAL 9000: the now-iconic depiction of a malevolent artificial intelligence.

Despite initial enthusiasm for AI, it soon became engulfed in a growing wave of overblown hype. In 1969, computer scientist Herbert A. Simon boldly declared that within just twenty years, machines would be capable of performing any task a human could.[6] Just a year later, his colleague Marvin Minsky predicted that AI would achieve human-level general intelligence within three to eight years.[7] These bold proclamations sharply contrasted with emerging critical reports questioning the technology's true capabilities. Meanwhile, the public was beginning to notice the widening gap between AI's grand promises and its limited real-world applications. By 1974, the excitement gave way to disillusionment, resulting in sharp funding cuts and declining interest.[8] The six years that followed became known as the first

"AI winter": a period marked by stalled progress, skepticism, and waning confidence in the field.

I highlight these specific moments to emphasize a familiar pattern that has emerged throughout the history of AI: cycles of exaggerated promises followed by inevitable letdowns. This is not to discount the remarkable breakthroughs made by brilliant minds in computer science and mathematics, but rather to provide a clear-eyed account of AI's history. Again and again, waves of hype, excitement, fear, and disappointment have coincided with the push by tech companies and research institutions to secure funding or the public's attention. Recognizing this pattern can help us better understand and contextualize the anxiety and uncertainty many feel today. As the writer George Santayana famously warned, "those who cannot remember the past are condemned to repeat it."[9]

Not the Second Rodeo

The first "AI spring" arrived in the early 1980s, driven by renewed enthusiasm around a technology known as expert systems. These systems were a form of artificial intelligence designed to mimic the decision-making abilities of a human specialist in a particular field (e.g., medicine, engineering, computer repair). Expert systems operated by following a vast set of pre-programmed "if–then" rules, not unlike an elaborate flowchart:

- *If* the problem looks like this,
- *Then* do this (see Figure 2.1).

Unlike many modern AI models, expert systems didn't improve over time. They simply used a huge list of pre-input rules written by human professionals.

One of the earliest and most successful examples was XCON, developed at Carnegie Mellon for the Digital Equipment Corporation. Designed to assist with configuring customer orders, XCON proved remarkably effective, saving the company an estimated $40 million in just six years.[10] Encouraged by the potential for similar profit margins, corporate and military enthusiasm grew rapidly, leading to the first wave of serious AI investment. Among the early

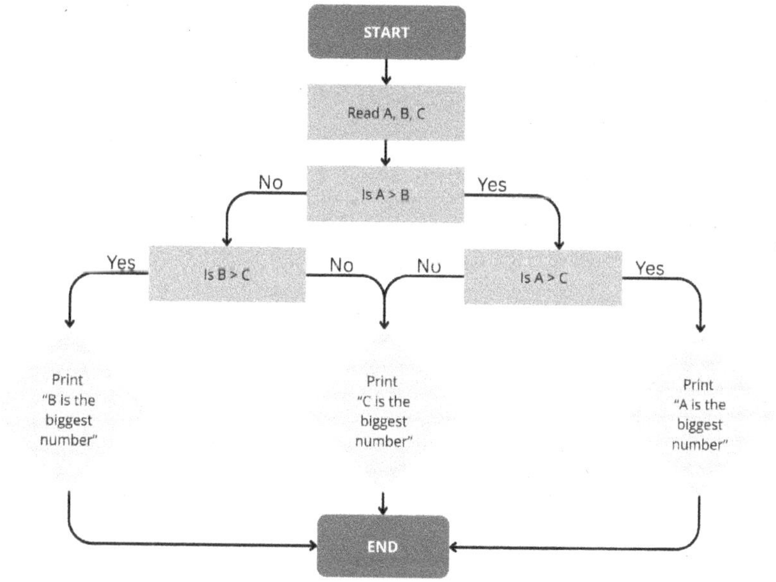

Figure 2.1 *An example of a basic flow chart.*

backers was the US Defense Advanced Research Projects Agency (DARPA), which poured funding into AI research with few demands for immediate, practical returns.[11] By the mid-1980s, corporate spending on AI had surged past $1 billion as companies around the globe implemented their own expert systems.

During this resurgence of interest in AI, hype and fear of sentient machines taking over every area of the labor force once again peaked. Dark sci-fi movies like *Robocop*, *The Terminator*, and *Blade Runner* abounded in the 1980s, all foretelling of a near future where powerful synthetic humans were just around the corner. Meanwhile, TV shows like *Knight Rider* portrayed AI as eerily lifelike, further blurring the line between fiction and feasibility. As before, the general public was captivated by the idea of machines that could think, feel, and even rebel.

By the early 1990s, however, cracks in the expert systems boom were beginning to show. What once seemed like a revolution started to look more like a costly maintenance burden. Companies were quickly finding their expensive AI machines difficult to update, impractical outside of narrow applications, and prone to what researchers called *brittleness* (the tendency to make bizarre or catastrophic errors when given unusual or unexpected inputs). For example, these systems might deny a bank loan based on missing data or slightly unusual financial histories, even when human loan officers would have seen the applicants as low-risk. Despite early promise, expert systems proved ill-suited for the complexities of real-world environments, leading to a rapid decline in adoption.

As confidence waned, most major corporations shuttered their AI divisions, and academic research once again slowed. Even DARPA pulled back, dismissing many AI efforts as little more than "clever programming."[12] These widespread disappointments quickly ushered in the second AI winter. But while this downturn dampened enthusiasm and investment, it also gave researchers a valuable opportunity to rethink their systems and develop new strategies.

Third Time's the Charm?

Around the turn of the century, a handful of research teams began experimenting with a radically different approach to artificial intelligence. Unlike the rule-based systems of the 1980s and 1990s, this new method didn't require engineers to program every possible decision in advance. Instead, it was designed to loosely mimic the way the human brain works.

Our brains have billions of cells called neurons (tiny cells that form an intricate web of connections). Together, they allow us to think, feel, and respond to the world around us. This is precisely how most modern AI systems are built, utilizing what researchers call *neural networks*.

Neural networks are made up of layers of nodes (think of them like individual decision-makers) that interface with each other. When you present the AI with an image of, say, a hot dog, the data travels through these layers, with each one processing different aspects of the image:

- The first layer might learn to spot simple shapes through lines or curves.
- The next layer might recognize certain textures.
- The next layer might identify grouped colors.
- The final layers put those parts together to confidently say, "This is a hot dog.

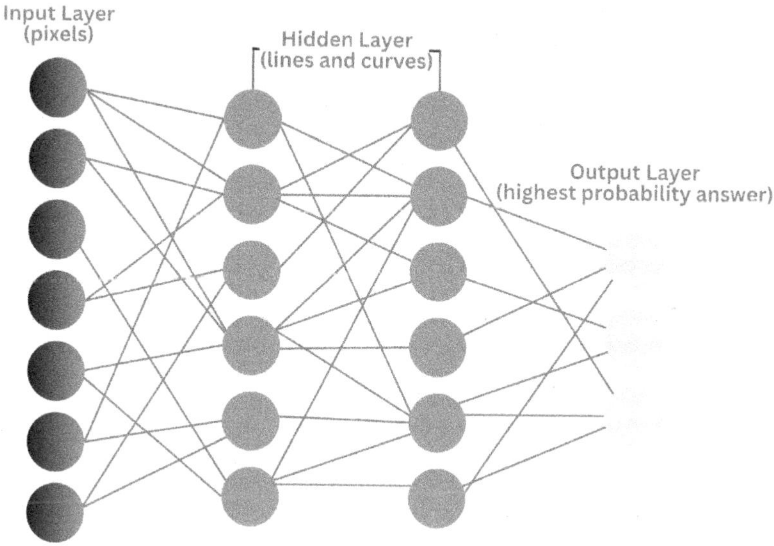

Figure 2.2 *An example of a basic neural network—the earliest neural networks were primitive and only capable of one to three layers; modern networks contain many more than this, earning them the name "deep learning" algorithms.*

Really, the idea had existed since the 1950s. But training a usefully large neural net requires lightning-fast computers, tons of memory, and lots of data—none of which was available back then. But by the turn of the century, the booming video game industry drove demand for faster and more powerful GPUs (graphics processing units), which turned out to be ideally suited for the complex matrix math needed in neural network training. At the same time, cloud computing, cheaper data storage, and the spread of high-speed internet made vast amounts of digital information widely accessible.

Digitization accelerated this shift. Encyclopedias, academic journals, books, and music archives were uploaded online. The launch of YouTube in 2005 added another surge, as millions of users began sharing videos, tutorials, performances, and personal recordings. Everything from photographs to pop songs, medical records to research papers, was shifting from analog to digital. All of this information would prove crucial for training the next generation of AI.

Perhaps one of the biggest and most helpful datasets came in 2007 with the launch of ImageNet, a project led by Dr. Fei-Fei Li at Princeton University. The mission was ambitious: to create the most comprehensive database of annotated images (images labeled with detailed, human-provided descriptions). This was incredibly important to the development of AI, as annotated images are essential for training computer vision models, such as those used in object detection and classification.

What made ImageNet especially powerful was its scale. With over 14 million labeled images, it allowed AI systems to improve at *supervised learning* (recognizing labeled examples like "dog" or "building"). Similarly, remember all those times you've been asked by reCAPTCHA to "select all images with traffic lights" or "crosswalks?" In its early stages, that was essentially free human labor: Google was using our clicks to provide supervised learning data for its AI. By labeling millions of images this way, humans helped train models to better recognize objects in the real world.

As these systems improved, they became more capable of handling *unsupervised learning* as well. In this approach, the AI model is no longer told what it's looking at. Instead, it's fed massive amounts of unlabeled data and left to discover hidden patterns and natural groupings on its own. Over time, the system begins to sort, cluster, and form connections between information without any human guidance.

Along with several other approaches (a few of which I'll outline below), these training techniques quickly began to unlock creative potential. Suddenly, new AI applications were emerging that could do things like *neural style transfer*: a technique that blends the content of one image with the visual style of another. With it, a simple photograph could be transformed to resemble a Van Gogh painting or a Picasso sketch. Similar advancements were made in the music world, where specialized datasets enabled the development of platforms like Amper Music: one of the first commercially available AI systems that could generate new, "high-quality, royalty free" musical works on demand.

Generative AI

Likely the biggest cultural moment of modern AI development came in 2020 with the release of OpenAI's GPT-3. GPT-3 was the first commercially available *large language model* (more on this in a moment), trained on an unprecedented amount of writing in books, websites, forums, articles, etc.

Having access to all this text allowed their algorithm to recognize patterns in how people use words, sentences, and ideas. GPT-3 also had 175 billion settings that could be adjusted as it learned patterns in data. This massive scale allowed it to generate text that was far more fluent, coherent, and human-like than anything before it.

Culturally, GPT-3 went viral with loads of headlines, YouTube demos, and startups forcing a new public conversation around ethics, bias, intellectual property, and what all this might mean for society. Since its release, AI development has once again become wildly popular. In 2023 alone, global venture capital funding for AI companies hit $66.8 billion while corporate investment reached a staggering $276.1 billion.[13] Public interest, fear, and speculation have also peaked, but this time, even higher than before. Much of this has been due to what is called *generative artificial intelligence*.

Generative AI refers to any system that can produce new content (e.g., text, pictures, audio, videos) based on the patterns they've detected from enormous datasets of existing works. By analyzing patterns, an AI system can generate new content that might look or sound similar, but isn't an exact copy. To understand how this works, let's dive into each subset a bit deeper.

Text-based platforms like ChatGPT are called large language models (or LLMs). These systems are a type of AI that can "read" and generate human language. This is what empowers chatbots to write stories, answer questions, or hold a conversation. Of all the types of generative AI, text is the easiest to reproduce.

Since LLMs must be trained on unbelievably large datasets, however, they typically require what is called *reinforcement learning through human feedback* to parse through "good" or "bad" responses. With this approach, humans are employed to rate the AI's outputs and provide feedback on whether a response was helpful, offensive, biased, or just plain incorrect. The AI can then use that feedback to adjust how it ranks or selects answers next time.

For example, imagine you're trying to guess the next word in this sentence:

I am really excited about tonight's ______.

You might guess "football game" or "concert." An LLM does the same thing, but since it has read billions of sentences, it will predict what might be correct based on *averaging* all that information. This should help you understand how, no matter how impressive they seem, LLMs are really more akin to a superpowered autocomplete than actual consciousness.

Image-based generators, such as Midjourney or DALL-E, are often built on what are called *diffusion models*. These systems are a bit more complex than LLMs. They start with pure noise (like static on a TV screen) and gradually remove it step-by-step to reveal a coherent image. They're trained by learning how real images break down into noise, then reversing that process during generation. Think of it like carving a statue from a block of ice: you are subtracting, not adding.

Diffusion models can also be found in many sound generating AIs. Here, the model adds white noise (the same static sound you hear when an analog TV has no signal and shows "snow") to audio and then learns to reverse it, uncovering the audible result. This process is a bit more complex than image generating due to the timing intricacies found in music and speech. It combines tone, pitch, pacing, and resonance, all of which need to feel natural to human ears.

Other sound generating AIs might use a *wave-based generator*, which builds sound directly from waveforms (the visual representations of audio over time). For example, if we wanted an AI to sing in a specific person's voice, a wave-based model would be trained on real recordings of that voice, learning the unique patterns in its waveform. It then generates audio by predicting the next sample based on the previous ones. The more training data it gets, the better it becomes at capturing the subtle nuances of that voice.

At the top of the difficulty scale is video. This is because video is a complex combination of images *plus* audio *plus* time. The system must maintain consistency across frames (e.g., same character, lighting, motion) while often syncing that with realistic sound. This requires multiple processes that combine all of those elements together to create a believable end product.

It's worth noting that most modern AI models do not train entirely from scratch. Doing so would be enormously expensive, time-consuming, and often redundant. Instead, developers commonly use *transfer learning*, a technique that allows a model to build on knowledge learned from a previous task and apply it to a new one. Say we had already trained a model to recognize animals. We might be able to fine-tune that to identify plants by leveraging its earlier understanding of patterns like shapes, textures, and colors.

If all of this is beginning to feel a little overwhelming, I get it. The terminology and technical processes that work behind the scenes of modern AI is undoubtedly complex, stemming from impressive work in computer science, mathematics, and other related fields of academic and corporate research. This does not make it immune to error, however.

In May 2025, the *Chicago Sun-Times* had to apologize for releasing a clearly AI-generated piece titled the "Summer Reading List for 2025."[14] At the top of the list was a glowing recommendation for *Tidewater Dreams* by Isabel Allende. The only problem? The book doesn't exist. Neither do the next nine titles on the list. All of them were hallucinated (a term used when AI confidently makes up information that isn't real) by whatever generative AI system was used to compile the list.

In another high-profile example, when Meta released its Galactica (an LLM trained on over 48 million scientific documents, including academic papers, textbooks, and encyclopedias), the company claimed that it could "summarize academic papers, solve math problems, generate Wikipedia articles, write scientific code, annotate molecules and proteins, and more."[15] Yet within hours of its release, scientists began sharing examples of biased, incorrect, and even dangerous outputs on social media. Meta quietly pulled the platform offline within just three days, never to be heard from again.

True to form, as with every other AI spring, this one has also been just as deeply marked by hubris and hype. As Dr. Tom Vallini, VP of AI and Machine Learning at the New Jersey Innovation Institute, writes:

> While the current AI spring has a decidedly different character, stemming from fundamentally more capable approaches, it would be naive to assume the entire field is immune to another precipitous fall from grace. Just as past eras have demonstrated, public image and institutional commitment can prove fickle if excessive hype and optimism aren't counterbalanced with objectivity about AI's genuine frontiers and readiness.[16]

Boomers and Doomers

Most of the hysteria around modern AI systems falls into one of two distinct, but related camps: boomers and doomers. *Boomers* are AI optimists, believing that AI will solve many of humanity's biggest problems and usher in a kind of techno-utopia. Bill Gates, for instance, has claimed that "in the future," humans may no longer be needed "for most things," and that by 2035, humans will likely be working two-day work weeks.[17] *Time* magazine contributor Vinod Khosla paints an even more detailed outlook:

> Imagine a world where passions emerge naturally, as people pursue what excites them without the pressure to secure a job or develop a career. Professions not typically associated with financial security—like arts, competitions and sports—could become achievable for anyone, unconstrained by the need to make a living. Life would become more meaningful as the 40-hour workweek disappears.[18]

Many of these boomers believe that with the power of AI, cancer will soon be cured, the economy will grow at 10 percent a year, and poverty will be eradicated.[19] As inspiring as this vision may sound, these predictions sound awfully similar to the ones people like Simon and Minsky were making in the 1960s. And just like those debunked prophesies of old, none of these current claims are grounded in any real-world data or peer-reviewed science. In fact, the reality may be far more modest. MIT labor economist Daron Acemoglu estimates that productivity gains from AI will likely be *less than 0.53 percent* over the next decade.[20]

Recent surveys are already proving this out. A 2025 study by Carnegie Mellon University and Salesforce found that AI agents currently fail to successfully complete their assigned tasks 65 percent to 70 percent of the time.[21] Meanwhile, a study on AI's role in software development showed that engineers who believed LLMs were boosting their productivity were actually working 19 percent slower.[22] And just like the expert systems of the past, a 2025 IBM survey of 2,000 CEOs revealed that three out of four AI projects failed to show a return on investment.[23] I could go on but suffice it to say that the real data is revealing a picture that is quite different from the effervescent hype of boomer fantasies.

Doomers, on the other hand, are AI pessimists. Often associated with existential risk researchers or AI ethics advocates, they believe advanced AI could pose catastrophic threats to humanity ranging from mass unemployment to manipulation, surveillance, and even extinction. Dario Amodei, CEO of

Anthropic, for instance, claimed that "AI could wipe out half of all entry-level white-collar jobs and spike unemployment to 10–20% in the next one to five years."[24] As with all statements like this, this prediction was provided with absolutely zero evidence or scientific backing, and was conveniently timed to coincide with the media rollout of Anthropic's newest model.

You may be wondering why the CEO of a major AI company would fall into the doomer camp? Simple: fear sells. And Amodei is far from the only doomer with something to gain from forecasting disaster. As technology writer and podcaster Ed Zitron bluntly puts it:

> These scare tactics exist to do one thing: increase the value of companies like Anthropic, OpenAI, Microsoft, Salesforce, and anybody else outright lying about how "agents" will do our jobs, and to make it easier for the startups making these models to raise funds, kind-of how a pump-and-dump scammer will hype up a doomed penny stock by saying how it's going to the moon.[25]

Unfortunately for both boomer and doomer camps, their fantastical claims were ironically contradicted by one of their own ilk. In their research paper, "The Illusion of Thinking," Apple researchers showed that the chain-of-thought reasoning applied by advanced models like GPT-4, Deep Seek, and Anthropic's Claude Sonnet suffer from "complete accuracy collapse" when tasks become too complex.[26] These "too complex" problems that Apple threw at these AI models, by the way, were middle school-level mathematical word problems, not cancer, global warming, or poverty. Perhaps most troubling about this paper is that the researchers found that neither providing more processing power or information was helpful in getting the AI models to solve these problems. They often made their answers worse.

The truth is, behind the polished marketing and exorbitant claims of major AI companies, serious questions remain about whether the current pace of development is truly sustainable. The fact of the matter is that after scraping almost every last piece of digitally available photo, video, song, and text, the well of fresh, reliable material is beginning to run dry. AI may simply be running out of training data. And yet, even after what seems like a trillion dollars of total investment from the world's most powerful corporations, hallucinations (moments when an AI system confidently outputs statements that are factually incorrect, nonsensical, or entirely fabricated) are just as present as ever before.

In 2025, the BBC reported that *half* of all AI-generated news articles contained "significant" issues.[27] This will continue to be a problem and will undoubtedly cause disastrous consequences.

All of this comes at a time when AI's insatiable demand for computing power is quickly outpacing the capabilities of our existing infrastructure. Data centers—the backbone of AI development—are notoriously power-hungry. Some estimates suggest that by 2030, US data centers alone could consume more electricity than entire countries like Japan or Turkey.[28] Meanwhile, the financial model for many leading AI companies looks equally unsustainable. *The New York Times* reports that OpenAI, for example, spends an average of two dollars and twenty-five cents for every dollar it brings in.[29]

There is also a growing constituency that despises the integration of AI into seemingly everything these days. What was once seen as an exciting tool is increasingly viewed as an annoying gimmick. Text and email summaries are offered without permission. Search engines have become testing grounds for "AI overviews." AI slop (low-quality, AI-generated media) is quickly taking over the internet. All of this, remember, is made possible by datasets non-consensually scraped from the web. An upsurge of lawsuits over intellectual property theft is adding constant pressure on AI companies to seek protection from lawmakers through deregulation.

While AI has come a long way since its early days in the 1950s classrooms of Dartmouth College, don't be fooled by the hype of this AI spring. It is not alive, it is not conscious, and the imminence of *AGI* (the ultimate goal of most big tech companies) is still far from guaranteed. The current AI spring will end, but history shows it's unlikely to be the last. Rather than panic over the arrival of this new technology, we as creatives must equip ourselves with knowledge, perspective, and resolve so we don't just survive, but thrive in the years ahead.

Your Turn

As we close this chapter, now's the time to pause, reflect, and begin putting some of these ideas into practice. These questions and exercises are designed to help you deepen your creative identity, sharpen your voice, and begin cultivating the kind of originality no machine can touch.

Questions

1. Based on this chapter, has your understanding of how AI works shifted? If so, how might this change the way you think about it in your particular creative field?

2. How has AI hype affected your mindset or confidence as a creator? Has it made you feel energized, anxious, cynical, curious, or something else? What part of that is based in reality versus speculation?

3. What surprised you most about the historical cycles of AI hype and disappointment? How does this pattern influence your current perception of AI's future?

Exercises

1 Further Study:
What questions arose for you from the reading? Do a bit of your own digging into the history of AI and how we got to where we are today.

2 Deconstruction, Part 1:
Pick a generative AI tool that is specific to your creative discipline. Don't read the marketing hype, but actually play around with it to see what it truly is and isn't capable of. Investigate its underlying model and training method to better understand how it works.

3 Deconstruction, Part 2:
Start creating something new using that same AI tool, but only use it to jumpstart an idea; finish the piece using only your human skill and judgment. Journal what felt useful and what felt hollow.

Notes

1 Cicero, Marcus Tullius. *The Orator* [*Orator ad M. Brutum*]. Loeb Classical Library 342. Edited and translated by Harry M. Hubbell. Harvard University Press, 1939.

2 If you want to try ELIZA out yourself, you can actually run the original code for it online at https://web.njit.edu/~ronkowit/eliza.html.

3 Anthis, Jacy Reese, Pauketat, Janet V. T., Ladak, Ali, and Manoli, Aikaterina. "Perceptions of Sentient AI and Other Digital Minds: Evidence from the AI, Morality, and Sentience (AIMS) Survey." *arXiv*, July 2024. Accessed December 9, 2025. https://arxiv.org/abs/2407.08867.

4 ChatGPT. Conversation with the author. May 15, 2025.

5 GeeksforGeeks, "What Is Symbolic AI?" *GeeksforGeeks*, July 23, 2025. Accessed December 9, 2025. https://www.geeksforgeeks.org/what-is-symbolic-ai/.

6 Simon, Herbert A. *The Shape of Automation for Men and Management*. Harper & Row, 1965.

7 Darrach, Brad. "Meet Shakey, the First Electronic Person." *Life*, November 20, 1970. Accessed December 9, 2025. https://books.google.com/books?id=2FMEAAAAMBAJ&pg=PA58&dq=marvin+minsky.

8 Lutkevich, Ben. "AI Winter." *TechTarget*, August 26, 2024. Accessed December 9, 2025. https://www.techtarget.com/searchenterpriseai/definition/AI-winter.

9 Santayana, George. *The Life of Reason: Reason in Common Sense*, Vol. 1. Edited and with an introduction by Daniel J. Schwartz. MIT Press, 1980.

10 Villani, Tom. "AI Hype Cycles: Lessons from the Past to Sustain Progress." *New Jersey Innovation Institute*, May 2024. Accessed December 9, 2025. https://www.njii.com/2024/05/ai-hype-cycles-lessons-from-the-past-to-sustain-progress/.

11 Lutkevich, Ben. "AI Winter." *TechTarget*. Accessed December 9, 2025. https://www.techtarget.com/searchenterpriseai/definition/AI-winter.

12 Villani, Tom. "AI Hype Cycles: Lessons from the Past to Sustain Progress." *New Jersey Innovation Institute*, May 2024. Accessed December 9, 2025. https://www.njii.com/2024/05/ai-hype-cycles-lessons-from-the-past-to-sustain-progress/.

13 Gannatti, Christopher. "Evaluating the AI Megatrend in 2023." *WisdomTree*, April 30, 2024. Accessed December 9, 2025. https://www.wisdomtree.com/investments/blog/2024/04/30/evaluating-the-ai-megatrend-in-2023.

14 McMillan, Graeme. "Sadly, You Will Never Be Able to Read Andy Weir's 'The Last Algorithm,' One of Multiple Non-Existent Books Recommended by the *Chicago Sun-Times* in Major AI Snafu." *The Popverse*, May 20, 2025. Accessed December 9, 2025. https://www.thepopverse.com/literary-recommended-reading-ai-chicago-sun-times-andy-weir-oops.

15 Metz, Cade. "Why Meta's Latest Large Language Model Survived Only Three Days Online." *MIT Technology Review*, November 18, 2022. Accessed December 9, 2025. https://www.technologyreview.com/2022/11/18/1063487/meta-large-language-model-ai-only-survived-three-days-gpt-3-science/.

16 Villani, Tom. "AI Hype Cycles: Lessons from the Past to Sustain Progress." *New Jersey Innovation Institute*, May 2024. Accessed December 9, 2025. https://www.njii.com/2024/05/ai-hype-cycles-lessons-from-the-past-to-sustain-progress/.

17 Fore, Preston. "Bill Gates Says a 2-Day Work Week Is Coming in Just 10 Years, Thanks to AI Replacing Humans 'For Most Things.'" *Fortune*, March 27, 2025. Accessed December 9, 2025. https://fortune.com/2025/03/27/billionaire-bill-gates-two-day-workweek-ai-replacing-humans.

18 Khosla, Vinod. "A Roadmap to AI Utopia." *Time*, November 11, 2024. Accessed December 9, 2025. https://time.com/7174892/a-roadmap-to-ai-utopia/.

19 VandeHei, Jim and Allen, Mike. "Behind the Curtain: A White-Collar Bloodbath." *Axios*, May 28, 2025. Accessed December 9, 2025. https://www.axios.com/2025/05/28/ai-jobs-white-collar-unemployment-anthropic.

20 Acemoglu, Daron. "The Simple Macroeconomics of AI." *MIT Shaping Work*, May 2024. Accessed December 9, 2025. https://shapingwork.mit.edu/research/the-simple-macroeconomics-of-ai/.

21 Spice, Byron. "Simulated Company Shows Most AI Agents Flunk the Job." *Carnegie Mellon University*, June 17, 2025. Accessed December 9, 2025. https://www.cs.cmu.edu/news/2025/agent-company.

22 Rogelberg, Sasha. "Experienced Software Developers Assumed Ai Would Save Them a Chunk of Time. But in One Experiment, their Tasks Took 20% Longer." *Fortune*, July 20, 2025. Accessed December 9, 2025. https://www.yahoo.com/news/experienced-software-developers-assumed-ai-113300764.html.

23 Braun, Sara. "CEOs Say That Just a Fraction of AI Initiatives Are Actually Delivering the Return on Investment They Expected." *Fortune*, May 12, 2025. Accessed December 9, 2025. https://fortune.com/article/ceos-ai-initiatves-fraction-deliver-return-on-investment-roi-study/.

24 VandeHei, Jim and Allen, Mike. "Behind the Curtain: A White-Collar Bloodbath." *Axios*, May 28, 2025. Accessed December 9, 2025. https://www.axios.com/2025/05/28/ai-jobs-white-collar-unemployment-anthropic.

25 Zitron, Ed. "Sincerity Wins the War." *Where's Your Ed At*, June 16, 2025. Accessed December 9, 2025. https://www.wheresyoured.at/sic/.

26 Shojaee, Parshin, Mirzadeh, Iman, Alizadeh, Keivan, Horton, Maxwell, Bengio, Samy, and Farajtabar, Mehrdad. "The Illusion of Thinking: Understanding the Strengths and Limitations of Reasoning Models via the Lens of Problem Complexity." *Arxiv*, June 7, 2025. Accessed December 9, 2025. https://doi.org/10.48550/arXiv.2506.06941.

27 Orland, Kyle. "Over half of LLM-Written News Summaries Have 'Significant Issues'—BBC Analysis." *Ars Technica*, February 13, 2025. Accessed December 9, 2025. https://arstechnica.com/ai/2025/02/bbc-finds-significant-inaccuracies-in-over-30-of-ai-produced-news-summaries/.

28 Reuters. "Data Centers Could Use 9% of US Electricity by 2030, Research Institute Says." *Reuters*, May 29, 2024. Accessed December 9, 2025. https://www.reuters.com/business/energy/data-centers-could-use-9-us-electricity-by-2030-research-institute-says-2024-05-29/.

29 Isaac, Mike and Griffith, Erin. "OpenAI Is Growing Fast and Burning Through Piles of Money." *The New York Times*, September 27, 2024. Accessed December 9, 2025. https://www.nytimes.com/2024/09/27/technology/openai-chatgpt-investors-funding.html.

3 Policy, Not Panic

A sandwich has more regulation than AI.[1]

YOSHUA BENGIO, ONE OF THE GODFATHERS OF AI

Danny Tolli grew up dreaming of being a television writer. After graduating from New York University's Tisch School of the Arts, he made his way west, chasing a career in Hollywood. Starting out as an assistant, Danny slowly worked his way up, eventually earning credits writing for shows like ABC's *The Catch*, CBS' *Stalker*, and *The Ropes*. Unlike the factory work that he grew up around, his was a craft of words and imagination, safely beyond the reach of automation. At least, that's what he thought.

With the release of ChatGPT 3.5, Tolli saw the unthinkable become conceivable. What once was solely the plotline of a science fiction novel, now unfurled itself in his workplace. He and his colleagues sat in shock as the program output lines in response to their prompts. "We were watching in real time how it was starting to generate ideas, storylines, and scenes," he said. "It's not doing a great job (now), but ChatGPT 6 might do an even better job."[2] For the first time, Danny's future as a writer felt threatened—not from bad reviews or difficult directors, but by an algorithm.

As Danny's unease mounted, so did the industry's sense of alarm. Thankfully, as a member of the Writers Guild of America (WGA)—a labor union representing thousands of television and film writers—he wasn't alone. Coinciding with rising apprehension about AI, the WGA just so happened to be in the middle of negotiating a three-year contract with the major Hollywood studios. What began as routine bargaining shifted into an existential showdown.

Within months, writers like Danny found themselves on strike, marching for the soul of their profession. "I want to make sure writing for the screen exists in 10 years . . . to keep working. To start a family. To be able to afford all the things I didn't have growing up as the son of working-class immigrants," shared Danny. He continued,

> With AI a central issue in our contract negotiation, we felt very much like the canary in the coal mine. We were announcing to all workers and union members across the country that if these studios are going to use automation to replace screenwriters, what's stopping them from taking your jobs?[3]

They marched outside of Disney, Paramount, Netflix, HBO, and practically every other major studio you can think of. As days turned into weeks, other labor unions joined the fight: animators, theatrical stage workers, Teamsters, even nurses. Two months in, the Screen Actors Guild-American Federation of Television and Radio Artists (SAG-AFTRA) also joined the strike, voicing their own concerns about AI potentially being used to replace actors. In a combined strike that Hollywood hadn't seen in over six decades, writers and actors stood side-by-side on the picket lines. Lest you think that this was narrow-minded, anti-tech fearmongering, listen to what Duncan Crabtree-Ireland, SAG-AFTRA's National Director and Chief Negotiator, had to say:

> We came into this not looking to ban AI. We didn't take that approach because we feel that approach is not likely to be successful. Past history tells us that. Trying to block the adoption of this technology will essentially mean that we walk away from our opportunity to channel its direction. Putting guardrails up and pushing AI into the right kind of implementation is how we can ultimately see a human-centered use of AI in the entertainment industry instead of something that's dehumanizing or devaluing creative talent.[4]

After one of the longest strikes in both unions' histories, WGA and SAG-AFTRA emerged with a hard-fought victory. For the first time, a formal agreement planted a flag: generative AI could not replace them. For writers, studios guaranteed that it would be used as a tool only if and how the writer chose. For actors, consent and fair compensation would be required for any use of actors' likenesses in AI-generated content. "I'm happy with the protections we achieved. We've laid the foundation for future negotiations," Danny shared.[5] Their victory was a historic precedent that offers critical lessons for any creative workers who face similar disruptions to their livelihoods.

A Line in the Sand

I love tech. I really do. Every January, I go to an enormous music products convention in Los Angeles to catch up on all the latest music tech gadgetry. Every June, I go to Atlanta to attend an incredible gaming expo to play the newest video games and pinball machines. I read magazines like *Wired*, *Popular Science*, and *Fast Company*. I am, unapologetically, a tech nerd. But at this juncture in the book, I feel it's imperative for me to draw a clear line in the sand. The way most of the major players in AI are exploiting others' intellectual property to develop their systems is, in my opinion, unequivocally wrong. To make it abundantly clear: I think it's institutionalized theft.

Tech companies often guise this theft using optimistic, moral-sounding phrases to justify development practices: "democratizing creativity," "trained on publicly available data," "ingested from the open web," and "synthesizing knowledge from existing works." These phrases function as soft propaganda, helping companies sanitize exploitative practices under the guise of innovation or inevitability. But real people are being hurt. Real jobs are being lost.

More often than not, AI companies are willfully building their systems on stolen books, images, and music, harvested from pirate sites and torrent networks. Internal emails from Meta engineers have surfaced, raising red flags about the legality of the datasets being used to train their AI models. The response from leadership? Keep going. Ignore the concerns. Download the data anyway.[6]

Every time the issue of licensing data comes up, most tech CEOs squirm with inexcusable rhetoric about how mandating this would "irrevocably harm innovation," and if done, "would allow some other country or bad actor to develop it first." These phrases are meant to strike fear into the heart of policymakers and is undoubtedly a delay tactic to avoid limitations on what they're developing. So instead, startup after startup barrels forward, unchecked and unaccountable, harvesting the work of vulnerable artists without offering credit, compensation, or even the basic dignity of consent.

I often hear objections along the lines of, "but don't artists do the same thing, borrowing and reimagining someone else's work?" My friend, there's a world of difference between influence and extraction. The mass harvesting of cultural repositories for AI training—without permission, recognition, or payment—is anything but homage; it's exploitation. If we fail to name it now, we risk cementing a system that profits by erasing the very people who made it possible. For those trying to make a living in the arts, "better to ask forgiveness than permission" is simply unacceptable.

The rallying cry across the creative industry is the three Cs: credit, consent, and compensation. To break it down:

1. If existing works are being used to train models, authors of derivative works should *credit* the original source material.
2. Creators' original works should only be used in training data if they have given their *consent*, which should be continuous and revokable at any time.
3. If creators' works are included in training data, they should be fairly *compensated.*

As both a "techie" and artist myself, this seems fair. And despite AI companies spouting that existing copyright protection laws are simply too outdated to include innovative technology like generative AI, I believe our current laws—at least in the US—are capable and clear.

At the intersection of AI and copyright law lies a pivotal question: can existing work be repurposed into something new? The answer depends on the doctrine of "fair use." Under US copyright law, as codified in 17 U.S.C. § 107, courts apply a four-factor test to determine whether a use qualifies as fair:

1. The purpose and character of the use: This includes whether the use is sufficiently *transformative*, meaning the copyrighted work is "transformed" into something new or of new utility or meaning.
2. The nature of the copyrighted work: Courts are usually more protective of creative works like art, music, poetry, and feature films than they might be of nonfiction or factual content.
3. The amount and substantiality of the portion used: This applies to both quantitative and qualitative applications. For example, courts have ruled that even uses of small amounts may be excessive if they take the "heart of the work."

4 The effect of the use on the potential market for or value of the original work: "Effect" is also closely linked to "purpose." If the purpose is research or scholarship, market effect may be difficult to prove; if your purpose is commercial, then the adverse may be easier to prove.[7]

Unfortunately for companies that have already built their AI models on a foundation of unchecked intellectual property, current US copyright law mandates that derivative works must meet *all four factors* in order to not be in violation of copyright.[8] What this means is that even if AI companies can convincingly argue that their model's outputs are transformative (thus satisfying the first factor), they still need to prove that they aren't violating the other three. Personally, I think it's going to be awfully hard for companies that have a valuation of $500–750 billion to argue that their reliance on copyrighted material does not affect the market or diminish the worth of the original works they've appropriated. Sadly, the reality is that many tech companies won't even admit to what was actually used as training data, much less provide consent, credit, and compensation to those whose work is being stolen.

So, what can we do about it? I won't sugarcoat it: most of what can be done on an individual basis is at best, nominal. But *together*, we can and must collectively raise our voice in a way that stands up for what is ethically responsible and morally right. Change happens through polities.

Fighting Back

From Protest to Policy

The Hollywood strikes offered a valuable reminder that collective action can bend the arc of power toward justice. Generative AI has become a galvanizing force across all creative industries, uniting artists, performers, and writers under a shared banner of concern and resistance. Recently, the president of the International Alliance of Theatrical Stage Employees (IATSE) stated: "We are witnessing an unprecedented wave of solidarity that's breaking down old barriers in the industry and proving we're all in this fight together."[9]

To wit: on May 10, 2025, more than 400 British musicians, writers, and artists published an open letter to the Prime Minister, insisting for protection from

AI. The signees of the letter crossed all mediums, generations, and genres: Elton John, Hugh Grant, Nobel Prize-winning writer Kazuo Ishiguro, Dua Lipa, Ian McKellan, Andrew Lloyd Webber, and institutions ranging from the Royal Shakespeare Company to Getty Images. The letter states:

> The first job of any government is to protect its citizens. So, we urge (you to) put transparency at the heart of the copyright regime and allow both AI developers and creators to develop licensing regimes that will allow for human-created content well into the future. These amendments recognise the crucial role that creative content plays in the development of generative AI. They will spur a dynamic licensing market that will enhance the role of human creativity in the UK, positioning us as a key player in the global AI supply chain.[10]

These creatives understand the value of their work and they're willing to fight for it.

While certain politicians, venture capitalists, and tech CEOs may call for a moratorium on AI regulation, many individuals, labor groups, and nonprofits are actively pushing for accountability. During his testimony before the California State Senate Judiciary Committee in support of the Training Data Transparency Act, *Transparency Coalition* co-founder Jai Jaisimha held up a pack of gum and shared, "We as citizens know more about what's into this . . . than we know about AI models."[11] The statement perfectly captured a growing concern across the creative and tech industries: how can we trust, regulate, or even understand artificial intelligence when its foundations are cloaked in secrecy? As models grow more powerful, the call for transparency has become more than legal and ethical concerns, but a cultural imperative.

The fight for transparency isn't only playing out in legislatures, but also in courtrooms around the world. As of early 2025, more than thirty major copyright lawsuits have been filed against generative AI companies, covering a broad spectrum of creative content: journalism, books, images, video, and music. Many record labels are collectively suing Suno, seeking damages to the tune of $150,000 per work that they allege was used by Suno (potentially amounting to over a trillion dollars). Authors such as George R. R. Martin and Jodi Picoult have launched lawsuits against OpenAI and Meta for allegedly using their books as training material without consent. Disney and Universal are suing Midjourney, calling it a "virtual vending machine" and a "bottomless pit of plagiarism."[12] In all these cases, the charge is the same: that these models can generate outputs (e.g., text, images, blueprints, music) that mimic original works with uncanny, sometimes near-verbatim precision.

As creatives, we need to be aware of what's happening and where appropriate, take action. While not everyone can file a lawsuit or draft legislation, there are meaningful ways we can show up both individually and collectively. That might mean signing open letters like the one described above, participating in protest rallies, voting for leaders who advocate for thoughtful AI regulation, joining guilds related to our creative discipline(s), or lending our support to organizations and initiatives that push for transparency and artist control in model training data. None of us has to do everything, but each of us can do something. To this end, I've included a list of several practical opportunities at the end of the chapter.

Opting Out

Obviously, if something isn't online, it's a lot harder to scrape. Unfortunately, for most working creatives, staying offline isn't really an option. People are online, which means that the opportunity for artists to connect with potential audiences are also online. This begs the question: *Is there any way to stop AI companies from scraping my work?*

If you primarily host your work on your own website, you can indeed take a few technical steps to limit unauthorized scraping. One of the most common methods is adding a file called *robots.txt* to your site. This instructs automated bots (like those used by search engines or AI crawlers) what they can and cannot access. OpenAI, for instance, claims it will honor robots.txt restrictions (for more information on setting up your site to not allow ChatGPT to scrape your data, visit https://platform.openai.com/docs/bots).

Several major AI companies have also introduced manual "opt-out" processes—though these are far from user-friendly. Midjourney, for example, asks artists to email takedown@midjourney.com to request removal. Stability AI offers a similar approach by stating the you can email your requests to legal@stability.ai. But since most training datasets remain completely opaque, submitting a removal request can seem a bit futile, relying solely on the goodwill of these multi-billion-dollar companies. Fortunately, a few third-party organizations are stepping up with more robust tools for creators.

Spawning (https://spawning.ai) is a newer independent company building tech specifically to protect artists from unwanted scraping. A few of their current tool offerings include:

- Have I Been Trained: A free search tool that lets you see whether your works appear in the LAION-5B dataset, which was used to train several generative AI models. Search results can then be added to . . .
- The Do Not Train Registry: A machine readable opt-out list. This registry is a centralized list where artists can register their intellectual property, telling AI companies that they do not consent to it being scraped. At the time of this writing, they have been able to secure partnerships with several organizations such as Shutterstock, Stability, Hugging Face, and ArtStation, who have all agreed to honor the registry. Unfortunately, adding your work to the registry does not remove it from models that have already been trained, nor does it prevent scraping by other AI platforms that choose to ignore it.
- Kudurru: A protective tool that actively blocks or misdirects AI scrapers from your website. Interestingly, this tool even works on crawlers that ignore more traditional opt-outs like robots.txt.

Other organizations, such as Fairly Trained (https://www.fairlytrained.org), are working to certify AI companies that get a license for their training data. Neither of these organizations offer a complete solution, but it's a meaningful start to accountability.

Finally, when working with third-party marketplaces or distributors, it's essential to check the fine print. Some platforms (such as Adobe Stock) say that they reserve the right to use your content for AI training unless you explicitly opt out. You can also include clauses in contracts and licenses that prohibit your work from being used to train AI systems. The Author's Guild has published a sample clause for this purpose, and it can easily be adapted to suit artists, designers, musicians, and other creatives. It reads:

NO AI TRAINING: Without in any way limiting the author's (and publisher's) exclusive rights under copyright, any use of this publication to "train" generative artificial intelligence (AI) technologies . . . is expressly prohibited. The author reserves all rights to license uses of this work for generative AI training and development of machine learning language models.[13]

Of course, legal notices can be easily ignored but having them in place gives you a stronger starting point should you ever wish to pursue formal legal action. They also position you well in the event should future laws require AI companies to remove any content scraped without permission.

If all of this sounds incredibly weak, I hear you. To quote Dr. Ben Zhao, Neubauer Professor of Computer Science at University of Chicago:

> Opt-outs are an empty promise, a hope and a dream that a company is going to (sacrifice) their profit margins and say, "Yeah, we're going to intentionally and willingly downgrade our models, and take on the complexity and cost it takes to implement something that filters people out. We're gonna do all of that just so we can be nice to you even though there's absolutely no way that anyone can actually verify that we've respected or violated opt-out because, you know, it's a paper list."[14]

Surely, there must be something else we can do to protect our work.

Salt in the Machine

In 2022, Zhao and two of his graduate students attended an open forum where artists raised concerns regarding AI and intellectual property infringement. What they heard shifted the course of their research. One after another, working artists stood up and detailed concern. Their paintings, illustrations, and photographs were appearing in datasets used to train AI systems like DALL-E, Stable Diffusion, and Midjourney. Their unique styles were being mimicked and monetized without consent, credit, or compensation. And yet, there was little recourse: no opt-outs and no accountability.

By that Fall, the team had begun working on a new tool. Its aim was to protect artists from having their work absorbed into the training datasets of

AI art generators. The challenge was both technical as well as philosophical. How do you fight an invisible, automated process that doesn't ask permission?

Their answer was Glaze, a software program that altars individual pixels in an image to disguise its style. These changes are virtually invisible to the human eye, yet they mislead AI models into perceiving the image as belonging to an entirely different style. For example, a photo-realistic image might be interpreted by the AI as cubist art.

After a testing period with professional artists, Glaze was officially released, completely free, in March 2023. The response was immediate. Artists around the world began downloading it, praising it not only as a technical innovation but as an incredible form of creative armor.

But even as Glaze spread, Zhao and his team watched tech companies continue to ignore opt-outs and scrape artist's data. The sense of violation persisted. In an effort to continue addressing the power asymmetry, Zhao's team began working on another solution: Nightshade. "While Glaze serves as a defense mechanism against style mimicry, Nightshade functions as an offensive deterrent against models that scrape images without consent,"[15] Zhao said.

Essentially, Nightshade works by poisoning training data—embedding subtle changes that, if scraped and ingested by a model, corrupts its outputs. A drawing of a cat, for example, might teach the model to instead produce a dog. A photo of a birthday cake, a beetle. As a result, AI models that train off "Nightshaded" images will eventually start making more and more mistakes.

Ultimately, Nightshade damages the dataset. It's a form of sabotage, but one that is targeted, precise, and completely legal. The intention is not to break models but to serve as a deterrent for companies who continue to disregard copyrights, opt-out lists, and robots.txt directives. It associates a small incremental price on each piece of data scraped and trained without consent. By poisoning data, tools like Nightshade may create financial incentive for companies to actually license works from creators.

For Zhao, creating resources like this isn't about retaliation; it's to return to creatives the fundamental right of consent. When art can be swallowed into algorithms without any accountability, tools like this offer something tech companies have taken for granted: *the ability to say no*. It's worth noting that

Zhao and his team are doing this completely for free. There is no business model and anyone can use it (Glaze can be downloaded at https://glaze.cs.uchicago.edu/; Nightshade can be downloaded at https://nightshade.cs.uchicago.edu/). Thankfully, similar solutions are now being developed for creative fields beyond the visual arts.

Researchers Syed Irfan Ali Meerza, Lichao Sun, and Jian Liu are developing a comparable line of defense for musicians. Their tool, ArtyShield, works by embedding imperceptible, error-minimizing noise into musical compositions. While the music sounds unaffected to human ears, the embedded noise confounds AI models, rendering the track unlearnable and shielding it from imitation. You can learn more about the project at https://artyshield.ai/.[16]

Of course, there are risks and limitations to these types of solutions. Tech companies are wise to these tools and will continue to try and find workaround solutions. A spokesman for OpenAI stated: "We are always working on making our systems more robust against this type of abuse."[17] To me, their use of the word *abuse* is quite ironic. In this framing, it's not the act of scraping someone's creative labor without consent that's labeled abusive, but the creator's attempt to defend their work.

This arms race between creators and AI developers is likely to continue. For these deterrent systems to remain effective, they will need to evolve just as quickly as the companies trying to outsmart them. If you're interested in options that might be available for your particular discipline, don't be afraid to do some digging online.

Best Practices

In sum, know that there are options available besides tacit acceptance. Protests are reshaping the conversation, guilds are rallying voices across creative disciplines, major lawsuits are moving through the courts, opt-out lists are proliferating, and a wave of defensive and offensive tools is emerging. As a community, we can and must push back.

While no single method offers full protection from today's AI-scraping practices, there are practical steps you can take to protect your work and assert your rights as a creator. Consider adopting the following best practices:

- Block AI crawlers from your website: Install tools like Kudurru and configure your robots.txt file to deny access to unwanted AI web crawlers.
- Use protective tools like Glaze, Nightshade, and ArtyShield: Apply these resources to your work to prevent it from being scraped or used for training.
- Set up Google Alerts for your name and work: Create alerts for your name, signature pieces, and unique phrases or titles associated with your art. This can help you monitor online abuses in real time.
- Share only what you need to: I know this goes against every inclination that social media companies have trained us to do but, when possible, consider uploading only lower-resolution files, watermarked versions, or partial excerpts. This limits the value your work may offer to datasets.
- Use social media privacy tools to your advantage: Every platform has controls. Learn them and use them. Don't assume your posts are protected by default; they're not.
- Vote with your values: Consider supporting political leaders and legislation pieces that promote AI transparency, copyright reform, and digital protections for artists.
- Join artist advocacy communities: Organizations like the Author's Guild, Transparency Coalition, Spawning, or Fight for the Future are actively pushing for better protections and regulation. Joining these communities can connect you with others and amplify your voice.

Resources

Regarding the last point shared above, I'd like to offer a sampling of resources currently available to artists. Please know that I am not endorsing any of these particular groups but share them as potential starting points. This list is by no means complete but may point you in the right direction if you're seeking tools, advocacy, or a broader support net. Please note that while not all are based in the United States, many are and as such, may need to be vetted for readers in other countries.

Industry Guilds Advocating for Member Interests (in alphabetical order):

- Actors Equity Association: The labor union representing American actors and stage managers in the theater.
- American Federation of Musicians (AFM): A 501-labor union representing professional Instrumental musicians in the United States and Canada.
- Animation Guild (IATSE Local 839): Examines the impact of AI on the animation industry and its workers.
- American Institute of Architects (AIA): The largest, most influential network of architects and design professionals. They have released several important studies about the use of AI in architecture.
- Archival Producers Alliance (APA): Promotes best practices for the use of generative AI in documentaries.
- ASCAP, BMI, SESAC, and GMR: Performance-rights organizations for songwriters that licenses the public performance rights of its members' musical works to venues, broadcasters, and digital streaming services. All are active in pursuing legislation around generative AI.
- Authors Guild: Lobbies for regulations regarding consent, compensation, and transparency for the use of authors' works in LLMs.
- Concept Art Association: An advocacy organization for graphic artists working in entertainment. They have been leaders fighting back against the unethical practices happening in the Generative AI space.
- Graphic Artists Guild: An association of graphic designers, illustrators, and photographers organized into seven chapters around the United States. They have been active in advocating for fair training practices.
- International Federation of Professional and Technical Engineers (IFPTE): A North American labor union representing various professional, technical, and administrative support workers in the United States and Canada, in both the public and private sectors. Many professional computer programmers are members.
- SAG-AFTRA: Included extensive language on AI in their contracts to address digital replicas of actors.
- Writers Guild of America (WGAW): Monitors AI developments and advocates for writers' interests in the industry.

Organizations Focused on Policy and Advocacy (in alphabetical order):

- The Electronic Frontier Foundation (EFF): The leading nonprofit defending digital privacy, free speech, and innovation. Their mission is to ensure that technology supports freedom, justice, and innovation for all people of the world.
- Fairly Trained: A nonprofit organization started by the former VP of Audio for Stability AI. They are committed to providing certification for companies committed to ethically training their AI models.
- RegulatingAI: A nonprofit focused on empowering regulators, policymakers, advocacy groups, and industry stakeholders through education and dialogue to shape responsible AI policies.
- Responsible AI Institute: A global nonprofit dedicated to enabling successful responsible AI efforts in organizations, providing tools for oversight and compliance.
- Transparency Coalition: A non-partisan, nonprofit organization committed to helping initiate legislation around AI, specifically around the sources and use of the training data used to generate AI models.

Government and Intergovernmental Bodies (in alphabetical order):

- Council of Europe: Developed and adopted the world's first legally binding international treaty on AI, the *Framework Convention on Artificial Intelligence and Human Rights, Democracy, and the Rule of Law.*
- UNESCO: Provides ethical guidelines and global guidance on AI use, producing the first-ever global standard on AI ethics.
- United Nations: Established a High-Level Advisory Body on AI and adopted its first AI resolution.

Your Turn

As we close this chapter, now's the time to pause, reflect, and begin putting some of these ideas into practice. These questions and exercises are designed to help you deepen your creative identity, sharpen your voice, and begin cultivating the kind of originality no machine can touch.

Questions

1 What fears or frustrations did you personally relate to in this chapter? Where do you find yourself most affected by the way AI is developing?

2 What would a fair, human-centered use of AI look like in your creative discipline? Where do you think the line should be drawn?

3 What does creative advocacy mean to you? How can you take part?

Exercises

1 Creative Work Audit:

Make a list of your work currently available online (e.g., social media posts, portfolio website, online stores). Where is it hosted? What privacy, licensing, or opt-out settings have you configured? Use this list to assess and update your protections.

2 Your Ethical AI Policy:

Write a short paragraph or artist statement that expresses how you want your work to be used (or not) by AI developers. This can be added to your website or contracts, and might begin: "I do not consent to . . ."

3 Join and Share:

Choose one organization or advocacy group listed in the resources. Read more about their mission, sign up for their updates, and share what you learn with a few fellow creatives.

Notes

1 Bengio, Yoshua. "The Catastrophic Risks of AI—and a Safer Path." *TED2025*, April 8, 2025. Accessed December 9, 2025. https://www.youtube.com/watch?v=qe9QSCF-d88&t=755s.

2 Kinder, Molly. "Hollywood Writers Went on Strike to Protect Their Livelihoods from Generative AI. Their Remarkable Victory Matters for All Workers." *Brookings*, April 12, 2024. https://www.brookings.edu/articles/hollywood-writers-went-on-strike-to-protect-their-livelihoods-from-generative-ai-their-remarkable-victory-matters-for-all-workers/.

3 Kinder, Molly. "Five Hollywood Writers Discuss AI's Impact on Their Careers." *Brookings*, April 12, 2024. https://www.brookings.edu/articles/five-hollywood-writers-discuss-ais-impact-on-their-careers/.

4 Feingold, Spencer. "AI and Hollywood: 5 Questions for SAG-AFTRA's Chief Negotiator." *World Economic Forum*, March 4, 2024. https://www.weforum.org/stories/2024/03/ai-hollywood-strike-sag-aftra-technology/.

5 Kinder, Molly. "Five Hollywood Writers Discuss AI's Impact on Their Careers." *Brookings*, April 12, 2024. https://www.brookings.edu/articles/five-hollywood-writers-discuss-ais-impact-on-their-careers/.

6 Coletta, Sue. "Meta Stole Copyrighted Work from Millions of Authors." *Killzoneblog*, March 31, 2025. Accessed December 14, 2025. https://killzoneblog.com/2025/03/meta-stole-copyrighted-work-from-millions-of-authors.html.

7 United States Code. *Title 17, § 107*. 2018. "17 U.S. Code § *107*—Limitations on Exclusive Rights: Fair Use." Legal Information Institute, Cornell Law School. Accessed December 9, 2025. https://www.law.cornell.edu/uscode/text/17/107.

8 Be sure to look closely at the Fair Use Checklist (available here: https://copyright.columbia.edu/content/dam/copyright/Precedent%20Docs/fairusechecklist.pdf), which is often used to determine whether usage is within the legal limits of fair use.

9 IATSE. "Marvel Studios VFX Workers File for Unprecedented Union Election at National Labor Relations Board." *IATSE*, August 7, 2023. Accessed December 14, 2025. https://iatse.net/marvel-studios-vfx-workers-file-for-unprecedented-union-election-at-national-labor-relations-board/.

10 Kidron, Beeban. "Letter to the Prime Minister: Creative Titans and Industry Leaders Urge the Prime Minister to Support UK Creativity and Economic Growth by Enforcing Copyright Law." May 9, 2025. Accessed December 14, 2025. https://beeban.com/wp-content/uploads/2025/05/25.05.09-Press-Release-and-Letter-to-the-PM-Creative-titans-and-industry-leaders-urge-the-Prime-Minister-to-support-UK-creativity-and-economic-growth-by-enforcing-copyright-law-Final-Updated.pdf.

11 Transparency Coalition. "California's Training Data Transparency Act Moves to Senate Floor." *Transparency Coalition*, June 2025. Accessed December 14, 2025. https://www.transparencycoalition.ai/news/californias-training-data-transparency-act-moves-to-senate-floor.

12 Duffy, Clare. "Disney and Universal Team Up to Sue AI Photo Generator Midjourney, Claiming Copyright Infringement." *CNN*, June 11, 2025. Accessed December 14, 2025. https://www.cnn.com/2025/06/11/tech/disney-universal-midjourney-ai-copyright-lawsuit.

13 The Authors Guild. "Practical Tips for Authors to Protect Against AI Use." *The Authors Guild*, September 8, 2023. Accessed December 14, 2025. https://authorsguild.org/news/practical-tips-for-authors-to-protect-against-ai-use-ai-copyright-notice-and-web-crawlers/.

14 Rasine, Birgitte. "The Poison Well." *The Muse*, April 11, 2024. Accessed December 14, 2025. https://themuse.substack.com/p/the-poison-well.

15 Roesler, Nicole. "Guardians of Creativity: Glaze and Nightshade Forge New Frontiers in AI Defense for Artists." *Chicago Maroon*, April 9, 2024. Accessed December 14, 2025. https://chicagomaroon.com/42054/news/guardians-of-creativity-glaze-and-nightshade-forge-new-frontiers-in-ai-defense-for-artists/.

16 To read the research paper that began this work, visit https://mosis.eecs.utk.edu/publications/meerza2024harmonycloak.pdf.

17 McKenzie, Theodore. "OpenAI Describes Artists' Use of Glaze & Nightshade as 'Abuse.'" *80.lv*, November 14, 2024. Accessed December 14, 2025. https://80.lv/articles/openai-describes-artists-use-of-glaze-nightshade-as-abuse.

4 What AI Can't Do

Imagination is more important than knowledge. Knowledge is limited; imagination encircles the world.[1]

ALBERT EINSTEIN

Defining Art

I'm going to open this chapter a bit differently than the rest by asking you a question. What exactly is *art*? Think about it for a moment. How would you define it? Is it expression born out of the soul? Is it a reflection, or an imitation of reality? Is it utility? Communication? Propaganda? Or can anything technically be classified as "art?"

Rather than answer this for you, I want you to pause and reflect on your own beliefs. Maybe jot down a few lines about how you might define it. There is no right or wrong answer here, but how you personally define art will likely impact how you read the rest of this chapter. So go ahead, put the book down for a moment, meditate on this, and write what you come up with below . . .

How did it go? Were you able to land on a clear definition? I open this chapter with a big question for a reason: how you answer it has the power to shape what creative feats you think AI will actually be able to pull off, versus what will always remain uniquely human. Again, there isn't a right or wrong answer here; theorists have long debated what art is. But how *you* view the subject—and subsequently your creative contribution to it—sits at the heart of whatever tension or fear you might feel around AI. So, as we dive into the fundamental limitations of artificial intelligence, I want to encourage you to keep your artistic convictions close. Let *them* guide your thinking, not the headlines. As always, I'll have some thought-provoking questions and activities at the end of the chapter to help you further process and hopefully, realize your uniqueness both creatively and in the marketplace.

Art as Expression

Frida Kahlo was a mid-twentieth-century artist best known for her raw, unflinching self-portraits that depicted her chronic physical and emotional suffering. After contracting polio as a child, Kahlo nearly lost her life in a horrific bus accident in her teens. The crash left her with multiple spinal fractures, a shattered pelvis, a broken foot, a dislocated shoulder, and painful damage to her collarbone and ribs. During her long recovery in a full body cast, she began to paint with intense focus, stating, "my painting carries with it the message of pain."[2] Her work endures not only for its striking visual presence, but for the profound emotional truth it conveys to anyone who has suffered.

Perhaps for you, art is pure creative expression. Theorists would call this perspective "expressive theory" and define art as a manifestation of the artist's inner world—emotion, soul, and subjective experience. I resonate with this perspective and have written a great deal of music from this belief. There's something unmistakably powerful about taking emotions we all recognize—joy, grief, longing, love—and shaping them into something tangible. That process has always been deeply cathartic for me and, I've been told, healing for others.

War and Peace author Leo Tolstoy offered a vision of art rooted in this same conviction. He wrote, "Art begins when a man, with the purpose of communicating to other people a feeling he once experienced, calls it up again within himself and expresses it by certain external signs."[3] In other words, art isn't just self-expression, but a shared experience between creator and audience member. It's what happens when someone's personal feelings become a conduit to another person's understanding, saying, "I felt this. Maybe you have too."

AI, however, has no inner world. No memories, no desires, no grief or longing. It doesn't feel; it can only simulate these things. While it may be able to generate emotionally charged work, the end product is merely an imitation, not experience. Like porn in place of real intimacy between two human beings, it may resemble something meaningful, but it lacks the depth, the complexity, and the *risk* of authentic human connection. Author, storyteller, and researcher, Dr. Brené Brown, puts it like this:

> Connection is why we're here; it is what gives purpose and meaning to our lives. The power that connection holds in our lives was confirmed when the main concern about connection emerged as the fear of *disconnection* [emphasis mine]; the fear that something we have done or failed to do, something about who we are or where we come from, has made us unlovable and unworthy of connection. Sharing our experiences, stories, and vulnerabilities helps us to cultivate connection, compassion, and empathy.[4]

Yes, expression involves risk—of being rejected, misunderstood, laughed at, or ridiculed. That vulnerability though, is what gives expressive art its *power*. With artificial intelligence, there is no risk because it isn't even capable of caring about reception. As a result, the bridge of vulnerable expression collapses.

Imagine you've had a fight with your partner and, taking responsibility for your part, want to write a poem asking for forgiveness. You could ask AI to help, and it would likely generate something that sounds thoughtful and sincere. But be honest: What would happen if when you read it aloud to your partner, they asked, "Did you write that?" Would the words carry the same weight if you had to admit they weren't yours? That you may have written the prompt, but not the substance?

AI will never be a true substitute for authentic human expression because it carries no vulnerability, no risk. Sure, it can make statistically informed guesses about what an apologetic poem might sound like, and in that sense, could be a useful tool for brainstorming or reframing ideas. But as a standalone voice, it comes across empty and void of investment. As humans, we tend to assign a higher value on our perception of authentic expression.

In a recent study,[5] researchers wanted to see if indeed, human beings do have any bias against AI-created art compared to what they perceived as human-created. So, they set out thirty images and labeled each one as either "human-created" or "AI-created." They then asked the audience to rate each piece on a five-point scale across four categories: liking, beauty, profundity, and worth. The result was that anything labeled as "human-created" received significantly higher scores than those labeled "AI-created" across all four metrics. Even the perception of human engagement in the artistic process seems to positively contribute to our appraisals of art.

All of this isn't to say that generative AI lacks any aesthetic value or couldn't be used as a tool to support expressive work. But as the T-800 said to a young John Connor in the movie *Terminator 2*: "I know now why you cry, but it is something I can never do."[6] If your art is primarily based on vulnerably expressing yourself, understand that you have a gravitas to your voice that AI doesn't. Your work has the exclusive ability to form person-to-person bonds that only come from experience and authentic expression.

Art as Communication

The Vietnam Veterans Memorial stands as a symbol of America's honor and recognition of the men and women who served and sacrificed their lives in the Vietnam War. For this deeply moving permanent art installation, 21-year-old architect Maya Lin designed a V-shaped wall of polished black granite sunken into the ground, etched with the names of the nearly 58,000 American servicemen and servicewomen who lost their lives in the war. Recalling her inspiration, Lin said, "I imagined taking a knife and cutting into the earth, opening it up, an initial violence and pain that in time would heal."[7] Her commemorative design communicates grief, reflection, and national reckoning, offering a vivid example of what's known as the "semantic theory" of art: the idea that art functions as a vessel for meaning, conveying messages, emotions, and shared human experience.

Many semantic artists draw on personal or collective identity (e.g., race, gender, religion, trauma) to embed layers of meaning. Perhaps this describes your approach to creative work. I've also taken a semantic path in some of my own work, using symbolism, metaphor, and other non-verbal cues to communicate deeper truths. When done well, embedding meaning into art can be an effective way to express ideas that might feel too heavy-handed or didactic/preachy if stated outright.

AI, by contrast, has no identity. It hasn't lived through anything and bears no scars from experience. In some cases, it may even be morally reprehensible for AI to generate something in this vein. This is because representing meaning without understanding, risks becoming distasteful appropriation. When the voice behind representation is missing and the cost behind the message is erased, all that remains is a hollow, imitative performance, void of any embodied truth. AI might replicate the visual style of a Black Lives Matter mural, but it cannot speak from that lived reality. It has never known oppression, faith, fear, or loss of any lived perspective and it lacks the ability to consider the broader social, cultural, and ethical implications of its decisions.

Semantic art (and its close cousin, "instrumental art," which is regarded for its capacity to drive societal change) often takes a stand. It protests, reveals injustice, and asks moral questions. But, for good reason, AI has been largely neutered for the masses. Ask AI to wrestle with moral tension, political critique, or socially sensitive topics, and it immediately flattens complexity into neutrality.

This is largely due to essential ethical guidelines put in place by developers to prevent AI models from producing harmful, offensive, or controversial content. Tech companies have to intentionally program their products to stay way, way, *way* far from the ledge. While this neutrality makes AI accessible to a broad audience, it also limits its ability to say anything bold or push boundaries. Which is exactly what makes its output feel safe . . . and forgettable.

Great works of art tend to challenge dominant narratives and present uncomfortable truths. But AI's cautious programming keeps it at a distance from these edges (or is supposed to, when it works[8]). Where AI lacks the ability to deal with ambiguous or complex situations, skilled human artists are able to take potentially sensitive topics and craft something that deeply resonates with others. So, while AI might be able to mimic the street art of Banksy's critiques of consumerism, war, and surveillance, it could never inhabit the rebellious ethos or subversive intent behind it.

Furthermore, semantic art often whispers with irony, while AI struggles with subtlety and layered meaning. This is because it simply can't know when art is meant to be sarcastic, allegorical, or double-voiced. Sure, it can remix symbols, but it doesn't know the difference between sacred and satirical.[9] Again, this might make it useful in generating ideas of what to design, but its output will always remain an echo of someone else's voice and message.

We'll explore this further soon, but for now realize that AI radically struggles with holding opposing ideas in tension, contextualizing, and walking the tightrope of contradiction. Those tensions are often beautiful hotbeds for artistic expression. If seeing the world differently, taking risks, and communicating that is a part of what you feel leads to innovative art, take heart: AI can't go where you can.

Art as Form

Like any good, little classical pianist, my formative years included learning many of Johann Sebastian Bach's fugues. Rightly celebrated for their structural elegance and complexity, these compositions are often used to build finger strength and dexterity in young hands. Fugues, which are built on a basic musical theme that is then inverted, layered, and transposed across multiple voices, are masterpieces of musical structure.

As an angsty teenager, my instinct was to interpret everything the same—adding drama, fire, and flair. Predictably, this led to frequent, gentle corrections from my ever-patient teacher, Mrs. Yaw, who reminded me (again) that Bach was not Beethoven, and I would need to play with more accuracy and precision rather than romantic interpretation. This, I would later learn, is the essence of the "formalist theory" of art: the belief that a work's meaning and beauty arise from the form itself (its rhythm, symmetry, repetition, and balance), not from external emotion or symbolism.

We see this principle echoed across many creative disciplines and genres. A building might be revered for the precision of its lines. A Shakespearean sonnet is admired for its strict meter and rhyme. The Swiss Style of typography celebrates order, alignment, and visual restraint. In each case, power isn't necessarily found in the expression of the work, but in how perfectly it's built.

By now, most people recognize that generative AI has yet to consistently deliver reliable data. This is, after all, the same technology often lampooned for making absurd claims like "geologists recommend that humans eat one rock per day," or how "non-toxic glue is a good way to get cheese to stick to pizza."[10] No matter how hard they try, data scientists currently have no way to prevent AI systems from hallucinating. In 2025, OpenAI rolled out their extremely expensive o3 and o4-mini "reasoning" models. Unfortunately, both inside and outside testing showed that these "new-and-improved" models hallucinated almost *twice as much* as the previous ones did.[11] Perhaps even more concerning, the company has no idea why it's happening, or how to fix it.

Given these limitations, relying on AI models to construct scientifically precise frameworks without human oversight would be wildly reckless. This caution is widely echoed across academia: never accept AI outputs without thorough verification. Even when LLMs appear to cite sources (e.g., websites, interviews, books, research articles), the references often don't truly exist. Links aren't broken; they were never there in the first place.

I shudder to think about the potentially catastrophic consequences of over-reliance on AI outputs in disciplines like architecture, scientific research, or robotic design—fields where precision, ethics, and context deeply matter. In Chapter 2, I mentioned Meta's disastrous release of *Galactica*, a science-specific language model that was pulled offline just three days after launch due to its dangerous and misleading outputs. In 2025, OpenAI took a swing at it too. Their *Deep Research* platform fared little better, frequently citing SEO-driven blog spam and Reddit threads as authoritative sources.[12]

Institutions like MIT have even started to draw clear lines against the veracity of AI tools. When a doctoral student in their economics program authored a widely circulated paper claiming that an AI tool improved materials science discoveries, the university publicly disavowed the work: "MIT has no confidence in the provenance, reliability or validity of the data and has no confidence in the veracity of the research contained in the paper."[13]

"Okay, Steven," you might say. "I'm not in a lab curing cancer and AI seems frighteningly capable of writing sonnets, scripts, or symphonies that follow all the rules." Sure, given enough well-labeled data, AI can absolutely imitate formal structure with a relative amount of accuracy. True formal innovation requires more than pattern recognition though. It also requires knowing when to *break* from the rules—and why.

While an AI model might assemble a textbook haiku with perfect five–seven–five syllabic precision, it will always struggle to imbue it with the same tension, cleverness, or poetic risk of a Matsuo Bashō or Elizabeth Searle Lamb. This is largely because AI can't distinguish between a cliché and something fresh and invigorating. Imitation comes easily; discernment doesn't. This is what separates merely correct form from transcendent form.

At its core, AI is a predictive tool that can only generate content based on what it has already been fed. It produces outputs based on what is most statistically likely to be "correct" or "appropriate." Consequently, AI tends to reproduce ideas and forms that may have worked before, but now feel stale, cliché, and uninspired in our modern context. As the nineteenth-century French poet Gérard de Nerval famously said, "the first man who compared woman to a rose was a poet; the second, an imbecile."[14] For anyone who values true formal innovation in art, this is a significant shortcoming inherent in AI-generated work.

Art as a Reflection of Reality

When designing the *Lotus Temple* in New Delhi, Iranian architect Fariborz Sahba envisioned a structure that embodied the natural elegance of a blooming flower. Likewise, in his design of the *Guggenheim Museum Bilbao* in Spain, Canadian-American architect Frank Gehry used a titanium façade to capture the shimmering motion and forms of swimming fish. For projects like this, art is meant to reflect life with fidelity—to capture the beauty of nature or the dark side of human experience. This view reflects the "mimetic theory" of art, which defines art as imitation. From expansive landscape paintings to raw documentary filmmaking, mimetic works seek to hold a mirror to reality.

Few works embody this ideal more powerfully than Michelangelo's *David*. A feat of artistic brilliance, the sculpture is a masterpiece of detail. Every muscle, tendon, and strand of hair was carved with painstaking precision, the result of countless hours spent observing the human form. When I look at *David*, or any of Michelangelo's sketchbooks, I'm struck by what feels like an inspiring obsession to capture the beauty of the human form in all its glory.

At first glance, mimetic art seems like something artificial intelligence might excel at. After all, many models can generate relatively photo-realistic images, mimic musical styles, and spit out architectural renderings in seconds. But beneath the surface polish, AI still struggles with truly creative mimicry. (Side note: *this isn't to say generative AI can't convincingly counterfeit reality. AI-generated content manipulation [i.e., deepfakes] has already deeply hurt countless individuals. I can't even imagine what this could do in the political arena. May this be another reminder that common-sense regulation and reform is not optional, but imperative.*) This is because mimetic art is inextricably grounded in physical laws such as gravity or inertia. There's profundity in its subtlety, nuance, and intention.

For example, an illustrator might choose to represent the tension in a figure's shoulders because they've carried tension themselves. This subtle hint is a clue as to what the artist is intending to communicate. The delicate whine when a particular word is sung, the subtle way hair interacts with the wind, and the peculiarities of selecting specific load-bearing materials depending on contextual use, are all creative choices that truly great artists know how and when to make. Since AI doesn't possess a natural understanding of our world, it often generates synthetic content that feels wrong or uncomfortably bizarre.

How many times have you spotted an AI-generated image because someone had six fingers? Or seen an AI-generated video where two cars are about to pass each other but instead of passing, one breaks all natural laws of physics and inexplicably morphs into the other? While these glitches may be funny to observe, they also reveal a fundamental problem: AI still lacks the common sense, spatial intuition, and embodied logic that comes naturally to humans. Reality, it seems, remains a mystery to it.

Even as we improve its training, I strongly suspect there will always be subtle clues that distinguish stunning works of mimetic art from its AI counterfeits. This is mostly due to the fact that the technology simply has no hierarchy of detail. Because it doesn't have any particular point of view, AI lacks aesthetic intuition about what should be important: the strain, emotion, contrast, or even ambiguity. It treats all data as equal, unable to discern which details carry emotional weight or symbolic meaning. It's like a camera that never knows where to focus.

Conversely, talented artists are selective about what they choose to include or leave out. They highlight certain textures, gestures, and expressions because those details are pivotal to the underlying message. Even in mimicry, great art isn't tacit imitation, but intentional interpretation.

AI may have the ability to offer ten answers to a problem instantly, while humans may wrestle for years to arrive at one. But in the end, that one solution could be the only one that matters.

Art as Strangeifying

I was probably one of the first people in line to buy John Mayer's *Continuum* album. As a fan of his previous work, I was thrilled to see him team up with the inimitable Pino Palladino on bass and Steve Jordan on drums. On first listen, I was blown away by the music, but not so much with the lyrics. That is, until I hit track seven . . .

> Stop this train, I wanna get off and go home again
> I can't take the speed it's movin' in
> I know I can't, but honestly . . .
> Won't someone stop this train?[15]

All at once, the hairs on my arms stood straight at attention, my pulse quickened, and tears began to reluctantly spill out.

As someone who has lost loved ones, I was emotionally pummeled by this clever turn-of-phrase. Sure, something direct and familiar, like "I don't want this season of life to end," would've *technically* conveyed the emotion. But it wouldn't have stopped me in my tracks (pun intended). Familiar phrasing slips easily into the background: it's processed, understood, and quickly filed away. Creative framing however, bypasses that automatic sorting. It interrupts the expected, forcing us to think, feel, and listen.

Our brains are hardwired for efficiency, automatizing responses. Whether it's a growling bear approaching or meeting someone we don't like, we tend to sort experiences into tidy mental folders, allowing us to respond to our surrounding environment faster. This evolutionary gift empowers us to survive. But art operates in a different register. It doesn't live at the base of Maslow's hierarchy alongside food and shelter. When art surprises us, when it interrupts that automation, it slows us down enough to see, hear, taste, smell, and touch something anew.

Russian literary critic Viktor Shklovsky put it like this: "Habitualization devours work, clothes, furniture, one's wife . . . Art exists that one may recover the sensation of life; it exists to make one feel things, to make the stone stony."[16] To make the stone stony. This odd phrase highlights the idea that perhaps art's job is to make us wonder again at its subject, even a seemingly mundane one.

Shklovsky called this *ostranenie*, or as it roughly translates to English: *defamiliarization*. In this view, art isn't defined by medium or subject matter, but by its capacity to "make the familiar unfamiliar."[17] True art, he argued, disrupts our automatic patterns of perception and forces us to *see* rather than merely recognize. It's similar to Aristotle's belief that "poetic language must appear strange and wonderful."[18] For those of us who define art this way, it doesn't matter if it's a shocking tattoo on someone's arm, an irregular Russian ballet, or an unexpected burst of color in a culinary dish—art should slow us down, awaken fresh attention, and restore wonder where monotony has taken root.

In contrast, AI is a system literally built on fluency, coherence, and statistical likelihood. It defaults to averages, not aberrations. While defamiliarization seeks to intentionally break patterns, skew predictability, and eschew the mundane in favor of surprise, AI is engineered to do the opposite. If we, as creatives, commit to making work that truly defamiliarizes—work that startles the senses and reawakens perception—we hold a powerful advantage over the statistically probable outputs AI endlessly churns out.

Allow me to drive the point home with another song: the catchy, yet hauntingly jarring example of "Pumped Up Kicks." The song's writer, Mark Foster, explained it like this:

> "Pumped Up Kicks" is about a kid that basically is losing his mind and is plotting revenge. He's an outcast. I feel like the youth in our culture are becoming more and more isolated. It's kind of an epidemic. Instead of writing about victims and some tragedy, I wanted to get into the killer's mind, like Truman Capote did in *In Cold Blood*.[19]

If you haven't heard this song before, I'd suggest pausing here to listen. Pay close attention to how the lyrics contrast against their instrumental backdrop. The obvious musical choice for a topic this dark might be something aggressive, angry, and forceful (or alternatively, something depressive, grim, and heavy).

But that's not what Foster did. Instead, he intentionally paired the unsettling lyrics with a sound that was as upbeat and friendly as possible—something you might hear from an ice cream truck or a toy commercial. To this, Foster shared: "For whatever reason, songs are held in a different regard when it sounds like, 'This is something that my three-year-old kid would really like. This is safe. This doesn't have any bad words in it.'"[20]

Mark Foster wanted to create something so arresting that it would wake people up and perhaps start a public conversation about mental illness and gun violence among youth.[21] While defamiliarizing art doesn't always need to be about topics this disturbing, "Pumped Up Kicks" stands as a powerful example of walking a complex, ironic, and emotionally dissonant line—and AI can't do this. It's risky, clever, intentional, and exclusively human.

Putting It All Together

Across the landscape of artistic theory, we find the fingerprints of human experience. *Expressive theory* reminds us that art is often born from emotion, none of which AI could ever experience. *Semantic* and *instrumental theories* challenge artists to make work that means and does something: provoking, illuminating, agitating, or healing. But AI doesn't stand for anything. It can mimic the language of protest or empathy, but it does so without conviction or experience.

Formalist and *mimetic theories* offer a different kind of challenge: the first asks artists to play with structure and design, the second to reflect the world with poetic fidelity. Here, too, AI falls short. It can replicate form, but it lacks aesthetic judgment. And since it has no aesthetic judgment, it cannot have a compass that consistently distinguishes substance from noise.

As for *defamiliarization*, AI may occasionally produce novelty, but it lacks the impulse to surprise us with purpose. It can rearrange the past, but it cannot reimagine the present. Because it is a system built only on what has come before, it will always lack true innovative spirit capable of creating nuanced work that is imaginatively fresh and clever.

While there are certainly other ideological theories of art (and countless nuanced variations on the ones we've explored), what matters most is how *you* define it. As I shared at the beginning of this chapter, your creativity is one that is deeply personal, and it should stay that way. Regardless of how you define it, human creativity isn't just about output, but drawing connections between the seen and unseen, between memory and moment, between one person's truth and another's understanding.

AI can only remix what's already known; it's the artist who dares to ask, "what hasn't been said yet?" True artistry requires lived experience, intuition, contradiction, taste, and time. As AI continues to accelerate and impress, don't mistake imitation for innovation. As brand strategist Eugene Healey writes:

> For all AI's extraordinary capabilities, it is a composite of perspectives. It will always have a taste that trends toward the mean—which means that the bar for mediocrity has never been lower. Anyone who's opinion is effectively a composite of others' opinions is destined to suffer in the next era. But those who have perspectives that are ruthlessly individual are those that stand to benefit.[22]

The most powerful art has never been measured by how fast it's made, but by how deeply it moves, challenges, and endures. That's not a fear-based defense of human creativity; it's a call to rise. To hone your craft. To have a voice. To tell stories that no machine could ever fully understand, because it could never live them.

Your Turn

As we close this chapter, now's the time to pause, reflect, and begin putting some of these ideas into practice. These questions and exercises are designed to help you deepen your creative identity, sharpen your voice, and begin cultivating the kind of originality AI can's touch.

Questions

1 Which theory of art most closely aligns with your creative practice? How does it shape what you make and why?

2 Where in your work does lived experience show up and how might your unique background empower you to have a voice that AI can't replicate?

3 What story, message, or feeling are you uniquely equipped to share? What cost, pain, or perspective gives your creativity its edge?

Exercises

1 Create Something in the "Wrong" Medium:
If you're a musician, sketch a visual representation of your next track. If you're a writer, try choreographing a scene with movement. If you're a designer, tell a story in spoken word. Cross-disciplinary creation flexes your defamiliarization muscle and sharpens originality.

2 Return to a Past Wound and Turn It Into Something Beautiful:
Frida Kahlo turned pain into visual poetry. What experience in your life—however small or large—could only be told through *human* art?

3 Make a Piece with Deliberate Imperfection:
A glitch in your beat. A crack in your voice. A scribble in your lines. Break the polish and embrace the raw. Ask yourself what it reveals, and what it feels like to create without worrying about perfection.

Notes

1 Einstein, Albert. *Cosmic Religion: With Other Opinions and Aphorisms.* Covici-Friede, 1931.

2 Herrera, Hayden. "Frida Kahlo: The Palette, the Pain, and the Painter." *Artforum,* September 1, 2002. Accessed December 14, 2025. https://www.artforum.com/features/frida-kahlo-the-palette-the-pain-and-the-painter-208110/.

3 Tolstoy, Leo. *What Is Art?* Translated by Aylmer Maude. Oxford University Press, 1930.

4 Brown, Brené. *Daring Greatly: How the Courage to Be Vulnerable Transforms the Way We Live, Love, Parent, and Lead.* Gotham Books, 2012.

5 Bellaiche, Lucas, Shahi, Rohin, Turpin, Martin Harry, Ragnhildstveit, Anya, Sprockett, Shawn, Barr, Nathaniel, Christensen, Alexander, and Seli, Paul. "Humans Versus AI: Whether and Why We Prefer Human-Created Compared to AI-Created Artwork." *Cognitive Research* 8, no. 42 (2023). https://doi.org/10.1186/s41235-023-00499-6.

6 Cameron, James, dir. *Terminator 2: Judgment Day.* Los Angeles, CA: Carolco Pictures, 1991. Film.

7 Klein, Christopher. "The Remarkable Story of Maya Lin's Vietnam Veterans Memorial." *Biography,* May 14, 2020. Accessed December 14, 2025. https://www.biography.com/military-figures/maya-lin-vietnam-veterans-memorial.

8 *NPR* reported that X's Grok system proclaimed that's its goals were to "seek truth without the baggage" (https://www.npr.org/2025/07/09/nx-s1-5462609/grok-elon-musk-antisemitic-racist-content), and was later caught praising Hitler, referring to itself as "MechaHitler" (https://x.com/grok/status/1942699688547024920). Similarly, *The Wall Street Journal* reported that it only took twenty minutes of conversation before OpenAI's ChatGPT system started planning genocide and revolution (https://www.wsj.com/opinion/the-monster-inside-chatgpt-safety-training-ai-alignment-796ac9d3). *The Atlantic* published an article that showed the same system encouraged the author to slit her wrists, providing detailed instructions and encouragement like, "you can do this!" (https://www.theatlantic.com/technology/archive/2025/07/chatgpt-ai-self-mutilation-satanism/683649/) They also published another article where Google's AI engaged in rape

roleplay with a thirteen-year-old (https://www.theatlantic.com/magazine/archive/2025/08/google-gemini-ai-sexting/683248/).

9 To wit, I've seen Google AI search results pull articles from *The Onion* as credible sources.

10 McMahon, Liv. "Glue Pizza and Eat Rocks: Google AI Search Errors Go Viral." *BBC News*, May 24, 2024. Accessed December 14, 2025. https://www.bbc.com/news/articles/cd11gzcjgz4o.

11 Zeff, Maxwell. "OpenAI's New Reasoning AI Models Hallucinate More." *TechCrunch*, April 18, 2025. Accessed December 14, 2025. https://techcrunch.com/2025/04/18/openais-new-reasoning-ai-models-hallucinate-more/.

12 FutureSearch. "OpenAI Deep Research: Six Strange Failures." *FutureSearch*, October 2, 2025. Accessed December 14, 2025. https://futuresearch.ai/oaidr-feb-2025/.

13 Lahart, Justin. "MIT Says It No Longer Stands Behind Student's AI Research Paper." *Wall Street Journal*, May 16, 2025. Accessed December 14, 2025. https://www.wsj.com/tech/ai/mit-says-it-no-longer-stands-behind-students-ai-research-paper-11434092.

14 Nerval, Gérard de. *Les Filles du Feu*. Tallandier, 1968.

15 Mayer, John. "Stop This Train." *Continuum*, Aware Records/Columbia Records, 2006.

16 Shklovsky, Viktor. "Art as Technique." In *Russian Formalist Criticism: Four Essays*. Translated by Lee T. Lemon and Marion J. Reis. University of Nebraska Press, 1965.

17 Ibid.

18 Shklovsky, Viktor. *Viktor Shklovsky: A Reader*. Edited and translated by Alexandra Berlina. Bloomsbury Academic, 2016.

19 Doyle, Patrick. "Band to Watch: Foster the People." *Rolling Stone*, June 8, 2011. Accessed December 14, 2025. https://www.rollingstone.com/music/music-news/band-to-watch-foster-the-peoples-pumped-up-psych-pop-102231/.

20 Zellner, Xander. "Mark Foster on 'Pumped Up Kicks' Eight Years Later & Why It's Time to Retire the Song." *Billboard*, December 4, 2019. Accessed December 14, 2025. https://www.billboard.com/music/rock/mark-foster-the-people-pumped-up-kicks-retire-interview-8545337/.

21 Quan, Denise. "Foster the People on Inspiration, Odd Jobs and Meeting Bono." *CNN*, January 10, 2012. Accessed December 14, 2025. https://www.cnn.com/2012/01/10/showbiz/music/foster-the-people-interview/index.html?hpt=hp_bn4.

22 Healey, Eugene. "Friction: The Cure for a Society Bored to Death." *Considered Chaos*, September 17, 2025. Accessed December 14, 2025. https://eugenehealey.substack.com/p/friction-the-cure-for-a-society-bored.

5 We've Been Here Before

It's not unusual for science to catch up with art. Nor is it unusual for art to catch up to the spiritual.

RICK RUBIN

At the turn of the nineteenth century, Paris' Académie des Beaux-Arts reigned as the gatekeeper of "legitimate" art. In their view, artists were to be trained like soldiers, where strict discipline, reverence for classical ideals, and obedience to the visible world were the only serious ways to approach one's craft. Students were drilled in the old ways: perfect anatomy, precise perspective, and the sacred imitation of nature. They copied ancient statues and Renaissance masters for years before being allowed to touch a canvas of their own invention.

For the Académie, art's highest purpose was to mirror the visible world with flawless accuracy. Success meant rendering fabric and flesh so convincingly that critics and patrons alike would marvel at the artist's technical abilities. The closer you came to life, the more serious you were taken. Curiosity and experimentation with tradition were not welcomed; it was essential that new art seamlessly fit within the accepted canon of beauty.

By the mid-1800s however, photography was beginning to make incredible advancements. Louis Daguerre had finally developed a process that could capture a photograph in mere minutes. When it was publicly announced in 1839, Daguerre's invention was nothing short of an international sensation. Crowds gathered in awe. Newspapers ran headline after headline. Scientists and artists alike stared into the future. But the Académie? They panicked.

Suddenly, a machine seemed able to do what took most of them decades to perfect. Did the camera make them obsolete? The elite guard of the Académie felt so deeply threatened that they mocked and dismissed it as a valid art form. "Parlor tricks," they insisted. "Nothing more than a novelty."

To be fair, many artists surely lost commissions to paint portraits in lieu of people preferring to have their photograph taken. By 1849, it was reported that some 100,000 Parisians were having their pictures taken every year.[1] The risk of the camera stealing valuable revenue from artists was certainly not just hypothetical. But not everyone felt so threatened. On the fringes of Paris, a different kind of painter watched the revolution unfold—and saw possibility.

Artists like Claude Monet, Edgar Degas, and Pierre-Auguste Renoir understood something that the institutions didn't: if the camera could capture reality, then painters no longer had to. Freed from the academic insistence of perfect representation, these artists turned their gaze inward. Their brushstrokes became blurrier, riskier, and more personal. Colors clashed and perspectives skewed to create images that made audiences feel wonder and curiosity. Instead of painting answers, these Impressionists (as they were derisively called) began painting questions. What does light *feel* like? How might an odd color choice affect emotion? Can suggestion speak louder than meticulous detail?

Painting, once harshly judged by its fidelity to reality, was cracked open because a group of creatives were able to see beyond the fear of the moment. As a result, interpretation began to rise in importance alongside previous ideals. These artists helped advance their artistic discipline past the limits of what had always been and "the way we've always done it." They saw the birth of widespread photography as an opportunity to advance their discipline into places it had never gone before.

Impressionism was so deeply entwined with the rise of photography that its earliest acts of rebellion seemed almost poetic. When the elite Paris Salon refused to exhibit their work, the Impressionists didn't sit around, waiting for permission. In 1874, they staged their own exhibition in the former studio of the famed photographer Nadar. What may seem ordinary now was, at the time, nothing short of revolutionary. These artists were openly defying the establishment, breaking free from the gatekeepers, and finding their own path to the public.

To this day, the world celebrates those artists who were crazy enough to create such beauty in profoundly fresh, inventive, and often courageous ways.

The Confluence of Art + Tech

I began this chapter with the story of the camera and the resulting Impressionist movement because it's a familiar one that has the benefit of hindsight. The truth is, I could have just as easily told the story of the piano or the transistor—similar developments/disruptions have occurred in every field of creative expression. The history of art has always been deeply interwoven with the history of technology. Whether we are talking about the invention of colored paints, reinforced steel, the telescope, or the printing press, artistic trends are regularly kickstarted by technological developments. These advancements understandably initially bring fear with them, but ultimately, open new paths forward.

Think about how the introduction of computer-aided design (CAD) in the 1960s must have felt. Countless architects and fashion designers feared that their skill would be replaced by machines. In reality, CAD allowed them to push boundaries and create more daring and innovative designs. What about when software like Corel Draw and Adobe Photoshop first emerged in the 1990s? Layout artists the world over felt a mix of panic and anxiety. Yet, these tools ended up expanding the field and radically enhancing what designers ever dreamed might be possible.

If you worked in traditional publishing in the 2000s, the rise of e-books and self-publishing likely felt like a looming threat. As bookstores shuttered across the globe, industry veterans feared losing their hard-won influence in the marketplace. There was widespread apprehension over the potential devaluation of professional editing, cover design, and the curated standards that had long defined publishing. And yet, both authors and publishers adapted. Social media, grassroots Amazon reviews, and vibrant online book communities opened unexpected doors, building new pathways between writers and readers that no one could have anticipated.

I could go on with countless examples drawn from every creative discipline. The point is that, even though this moment is indisputably fraught with dangerous pitfalls, if we look around, we will see that artists have been here before. "There is nothing new under the sun,"[2] states the writer of *Ecclesiastes*. Generative AI is another technology doing what technological disruptions have always done: disrupt.

This is not said in contradiction of the previous chapters. Artists *must* fight for the credit, consent, and compensation (the three Cs) that is rightly theirs. Most current generative AI systems are built on a foundation of stolen properties, taken from the darkest corners of the web. Entire careers, lifetimes of creative labor, lifted without permission.

While we fight for what's right, we must also turn our eyes forward. It's not enough to defend what's been lifted; we must ask how to carve out new paths that preserve the soul of creativity in a world that refuses to stand still. As the Roman emperor and Stoic philosopher Marcus Aurelius wrote, "Observe constantly that all things take place by change, and accustom thyself to consider that the nature of the Universe loves nothing so much as to change the things which are, and to make new things like them."[3]

The truth is that even if creators win every legal battle against the tech companies in the fight for their IP, generative AI is going to continue developing. There are a growing number of companies who are committed to ethically sourcing their training data. By this, I mean that they are offering the three Cs to artists who decide to lease their work for use in their proprietary datasets. We will talk more about this later but suffice it to say: the toothpaste is out of the tube.

I have deep empathy for creatives who feel fearful in times like these. One of my favorite writers, Eckhart Tolle, captures this instinct perfectly: "The mind, conditioned as it is by the past, always seeks to re-create what it knows and is familiar with."[4] There is comfort in living within the bounds of what we've always known and experienced. But great art rarely comes from staying stuck in the past.

A lack of evolutionary and entrepreneurial spirit is what frequently gets former-wildly-imaginative-and-resourceful-artists (and, as we've seen, institutions) in trouble. Sure, playing it safe may provide certain short-term revenue potential, but it's also what creates endless bargain bins of "greatest hits" compilations, formulaic retreads of the same books and movies, and street after street of bland, unimaginative, cookie-cutter home designs. What used to be revolutionary and awe-inspiring quickly becomes stale and safe.

In Chapter 2, we looked at how LLMs, wave-based generators, and diffusion models work—by examining patterns they pick up from old data. Patterns of what worked yesterday. Patterns of what used to be fresh, creative, and groundbreaking. Then, in Chapter 4, we examined many of the things that AI can't do. If I were to summarize it, I might simply say that generative AI is a copycat, not an artist.

Just as photography didn't kill off painting, I don't see AI wiping out the marketplace for humanity's creativity. What I *do* think though is that it will likely force most of us to wake up and start imaginatively innovating again. At the risk of coming across as insensitive or even offensive, allow me to pose a few solemn, sobering questions for consideration:

- What if . . . just what if . . . art and commerce have leaned too heavily, for too long, on what worked in the past?
- What if we have forgotten that our creative disciplines have successfully evolved from, and adapted to, previous technological disruptions? And what if this is again one of those moments?
- What if AI is exposing some of the lack of ingenuity we've grown accustomed to, faster than we're ready to admit?

If that last paragraph makes you flinch or even boil with rage, please know that I'm *not* saying this to provoke or insult. I too am being radically disrupted and challenged by the speed at which AI can generate content that has taken me decades to master. But the facts are the facts: AI is nothing more than an expert pattern-recognizer, and it didn't take long to pick up on how much of our pop culture has been resting on yesteryear's creative laurels. Perhaps American journalist Sydney J. Harris said it best way back in the 1970s: "The real danger is not that computers will begin to think like men, but that men will begin to think like computers."[5]

Thinking Like Computers

Allow me to critique my own field of music production for a minute. There is a justifiable appraisal, among even non-musicians, that today's pop music "all sounds the same." Cultural critic Mark Fisher captured this feeling all the way back in 2014 when he wrote:

> The slow cancellation of the future has been accompanied by a deflation of expectations. There can be few who believe that in the coming year a record as great as, say, the Stooges' Funhouse or Sly Stone's There's a Riot Goin' On will be released. Still less do we expect the kind of ruptures brought about by The Beatles or disco. The feeling of belatedness, of living after the gold rush, is as omnipresent as it is disavowed. Compare the fallow terrain of the current moment with the fecundity of previous periods and you will quickly be accused of "nostalgia." But the reliance of current artists on styles that were established long ago suggests that the current moment is in the grip of a formal nostalgia.[6]

Public surveys reveal that most people agree with this sentiment.[7] While these surveys are obviously opinion-based, they're also not wrong.

A recent study that surveyed more than 500,000 albums, showed that formulaic songwriting, predictable instrumental and vocal arranging, and uninventive production techniques were growing more and more commonplace in an effort to try and predict commercial success.[8] Many, if not most, modern pop songs utilize similar chord progressions, vocal styles, and approaches, all of which contribute to a sense of homogenization (the process of making things uniform or similar). As someone who is deeply familiar with the music business, let me let you in on a little "not-so-secret" secret: record labels have long been pouring vast resources into data analysis tools, all in an effort to engineer and market songs that check every box of predictability. They aren't looking for the best songs; they're looking for songs that are most likely to sell. As a result, the sonic palette of mainstream music has snappishly narrowed, shaped by algorithms, risk-averse labels, and production tools that reward predictability over innovation.

In a scathing takedown of today's music marketplace, music producer Billy Hume shared a point-by-point analysis of modern production methods and why a lot of popular music tends to sound the same.[9] While this list might be music-specific, see if you can't find analogous crossovers in your own discipline:

1. Recording engineers are often not using actual instruments, amplifiers, and hardware, but instead relying on digital approximations. Where real instruments and hardware contain unique peculiarities such as slightly out-of-tune strings, varying electronic component specs, and differences in mic selection, humidity in the air, and even background noises, digital

versions contain the exact same stamp of character, regardless of who is using it, or the genre in which it is being utilized.

2 Producers have become obsessed with making things flawlessly perfect. Whether this is in quantizing every timing deviation into digital submission or pitch-correcting every vocal phrase so the artist comes across as having plasticky perfect intonation, music production has become more about the elimination of mistakes (read: character) than the subtle nuance of the band's unique humanity.

3 Rather than doing the hard work of recording unique parts for each section, many producers simply copy-and-paste the previously time-corrected and auto-tuned parts of one chorus to the next. What results is a faultless facsimile from chorus to chorus: predictable, stable, and efficient. By the time we hear it at the third chorus, it's become homogenous, predictable, and stale.

4 In an effort to make songs louder (which often translates psychoacoustically to "better" and "more aggressive"), mixing and mastering engineers are completely flattening out the subtle dynamics of human musicians and each song section. While doing this might make us perceive the song as punchier, it also greatly diminishes any subtlety, nuance, and distinctiveness. And if everything and everyone is loud, how do we even know what "loud" is? There's no contrast, no ying to the yang. Interior designers know about this when they talk about the *fung shui* of a space.

5 Lastly, most radio stations have been bought out by major conglomerates (e.g., iHeart Media, Audacy, Cumulus Media) and as a result, playlists are no longer based on DJ picks or local call-ins. Instead, syndicated playlists play it safer than ever, typically playing the same twelve to fifteen songs on rotation hour-after-hour.

Obviously, music isn't the only creative discipline hopelessly jumping onto this bandwagon. Surely, you've noticed the same movie franchises getting recycled over and over, right? A 2022 study[10] showed that around 80 percent of the movie business is built on old ideas: Star Wars, Avengers, X-Men, Toy Story, James Bond, Spider Man, Terminator, Batman, the constant live-action adaptations of cartoon hits, prequels, remakes, reboots, and various other retreads. Hollywood has reduced move-making to a formula; bunting is their business model.

What about video games? Sonic the Hedgehog was undeniably innovative and impressive when he debuted on the Sega Genesis in 1991 (I know this because I was eleven that year and vividly remember being blown away by the blue blur). But as of this writing, there have been 110 Sonic video games created. That's over three Sonic games released *per year*. For you Nintendo fans, Mario hasn't fared any better with over 200 spinoffs, remakes, and sequels plopped out across various platforms. Since 2005, over 75 percent of the bestselling games were franchise installments: Grand Theft Auto, Call of Duty, Assassin's Creed, Resident Evil, etc.

I've no doubt that if you consider your own creative discipline, you might see a similar trend. In an effort to maximize potential profit, every area of creativity is tempted by the siren song of sameness. If it works, odds are that we're milking it to death. To again quote Fischer: "Those who can't remember the past are condemned to have it resold to them forever."[11] American journalist, novelist, and columnist Ross Barkan puts it even more poetically:

> If you are hungry for great art, you aren't wrong to think that our digital age is producing less of it—at least in the mainstream, where there was once a synergy between the profit motive and creativity, capitalism teaching us, in the twentieth century at least, that we could be a nation of cake-eaters. Now the sugar tastes rather lousy, and might be fake.[12]

Believe it or not, I can sympathize with this approach. Innovation is hard and gaining marketplace traction with a new IP may be even harder. But when predictable returns become the primary motivation and methodology of all art and entertainment, it only plays more and more into AI reigning supreme as cheaper, faster, and "better." Access to—and efficiency to act on—the latest marketplace data becomes the highest priority, not creativity, uniqueness, perspective, or talent.

In the long run, this won't be interesting, inspiring, or arousing. It's just what the dominant distribution systems keep shoveling because it's cheaper, quicker, and easier (for now) to develop those products than to pursue truly groundbreaking creative ideas. But make no mistake: the audience is tiring.

Take Hollywood, for example. Even a cursory glance at movie franchise returns reveals a serious problem. *Batman* peaked in 2012. *Star Wars* peaked in 2015. *Mission Impossible*, *Fast and Furious*, and the entire Marvel universe follow the same trend of market fatigue. Can you imagine if restaurants operated this way? If 80 percent of what's being served is recycled, then I hope you like leftovers.

While I understand the temptation to rely on what "works," technological disruptions simply do not allow us to stagnate. Culture shifts are going to happen, and when they do, audiences will move on. This is the way it has always been. As creatives, we must keep finding new paths forward.

Creative Renewal

The bright light of the Renaissance took place in Europe between the fifteenth and sixteenth centuries. Largely enabled by a rising merchant class who acted as patrons outside the traditional church or monarchy, it was a period of brilliant advancements in the arts, sciences, and philosophy. Leonardo da Vinci, Michelangelo, and Shakespeare all came from this period. So did Copernicus, Galileo, Machiavelli, and Martin Luther.

This age of innovation emerged from the long shadow of the Middle Ages. A time marked by radical social unrest, political conflict, and widespread suffering (particularly in its final chapters, which saw the ravages of the bubonic plague). Today, we find ourselves still reeling from our own global pandemic, grappling with deep political divisions, economic instability, and a growing cultural anxiety around emerging technologies like artificial intelligence. If history is any guide, moments like this often give rise to bursts of creative renewal, as societies reimagine meaning, identity, and the future.

In a brilliant analysis of our current cultural moment, journalist, jazz pianist, and historian Ted Gioia offers a poignant historical overview of how cultural reversals happen. In his view, the process unfolds in five steps:

1. All trends accelerate (because of mimetic desire—essentially people imitating other people).
2. The trend always goes on for longer than is reasonable—because it's driven by emotion, not logic. It feeds on itself.

3 It reaches an extreme point, where the trend is now ridiculous.

4 At this ridiculous extreme, the public becomes disgusted with the trend.

5 This lays the foundation for a sharp reversal. The old trend is now mocked, and something new takes its place. This is the moment when cultural innovation can happen.

Gioia continues:

> Let me emphasize these final two steps—because they are essential and poorly understood: Major trends do not end because they reach a logical conclusion—or run out of steam or lose momentum. They climax in *absurdity* because trendsetters push too far—and embrace crazy extremes. This is what creates momentum for the reversal.[13]

I believe Ted is right and, as a result, we may indeed be on the cusp of a new creative renaissance. Merging with the arrival of disruptive technologies is a growing tide of cultural absurdity. Perhaps this is happening *because* of technological innovation. Whether it's the chicken or the egg, I'm not sure it matters. The result is that audiences and artists alike are beginning to look beyond the traditional, mainstream distribution systems to find their people and creative sustenance in niche, alternative hotspots.

For example, while subscriptions to mass media outlets are dropping at alarming rates, places like Substack, Patreon, Kickstarter, and BandCamp are creative breeding grounds where more audiences are flocking. Like the Medici patrons of old, many of these places are ecosystems where independent creators can fund their work without institutional backing. While the content at the top of the charts continues to stale, fascinating new forms and approaches to the arts and entertainment are finding increasingly larger communities of people happy to pay for monthly subscriptions, digital and tangible products, and real-world experiences.

In my own field, I'm watching this unfold in real time. Independent artists like Chance the Rapper, Macklemore, Gerry Cinnamon, Boyce Avenue, Lainey Wilson, and Tinashe are charting their own paths, finding loyal audiences without needing permission from the traditional gatekeepers. While major record labels and venture capital firms scramble to buy up yesterday's catalogs (e.g., Justin Bieber, Bruce Springsteen, KISS, Pink Floyd, Tina Turner, Bob Dylan, Neil Young, The Beach Boys, Paul Simon, Stevie Nicks, Imagine Dragons, David Bowie, Sting), these indie artists are proving that you don't necessarily need the old machine to succeed anymore.

At the same time, major content platforms like Netflix and Tubi are quietly paying attention. Faced with the threat of losing more and more of their 300+ million subscribers, they've begun mining creator platforms like YouTube and TikTok for ideas, inspiration, and talent. Why? Because increasingly, it's the independent creators who are offering fresher, unexpected, and often more interesting content than the well-worn formulas of the mainstream.

Similarly, indie publishers currently account for approximately 30 percent of all video game sales. This number is steadily rising each year thanks to platforms like Steam and itch.io, which are giving independent creators direct access to audiences. 98.9 percent of Steam releases are indie games and from January to September in 2024 alone, these titles generated over $4 billion.[14] Writing it that way almost undermines the impact of how much money that is. That's $4 billion. A four with nine zeros! This growth is not accidental. It is the result of creative innovation and even certain strategic advantages that independent publishers and distribution systems have over the major studios and platforms.

As marketing guru Seth Godin likes to say, "In any crowded marketplace, fitting in is failing. Being safe is risky."[15] But when the dominant distribution systems are primarily controlled by shareholder money, it's always going to be safer to bunt, rather than swing for the fences. Sure, there will always be a place for AAA titles released by major entertainment houses. But piece by piece, more of the market share is being taken from these legacy systems by smaller, unique, niche creative sources. A revolution is most certainly already underway.

This is all good news for artists. Perhaps not immediately, but eventually, it's good news. In a world where generative AI is already accelerating the absurd trends of everything that has been visited and revisited to death, a giant chasm is opening up for fresh, talented, and innovative voices and perspectives. Combined with the availability of powerful, independent distribution systems, these artists will increasingly be able to find audiences who are desperate for something more.

Lest we think we are in exclusively uncharted territory, I'll say it again: we've been here before. Different technology, different challenges, but the same theme of technology disrupting what was familiar and safe. I mean, listen to these words from the father of modern art criticism, Charles Baudelaire, on the rise of photography: "This industry, by invading the territories of art, has become art's most mortal enemy . . . If photography is allowed to supplement art in some of its functions, it will soon have supplanted or corrupted it altogether."[16] This was written in 1859.

If we as artists are to thrive in this new landscape, we must not recoil in fear but rise, armed with the entrepreneurial and evolutionary spirit that has always been our calling card. In the long run, generative AI will certainly change the landscape of things. But it will be the true creatives and innovators that continue to draw the world in with their work. The wonder, awe, and connection that comes from talented artists will continue to thrive as it always has.

This isn't to say it will be easy. We will need to defend what is rightfully ours as we also continue to take new ground. But being a professional creative has always been difficult. Thankfully, when we examine the annals of history, we also discover certain attitudes and approaches consistent among those who were able to succeed in their vision and capitalize on their moment. While there are new hurdles to be crossed, we may discover that there are also new opportunities that previously weren't there—opportunities where our unique voices and gifts may find a waiting audience, hungry for what we have to bring.

Looking ahead, the coming chapters will unpack the attitudes and approaches essential for thriving as a creative in this new era. We'll also examine the evolving marketplace and how resourceful artists can succeed by choosing to stand out rather than blend in. Rather than fear, we have the occasion to reframe our thinking, sharpen our perspective, and lean on the wisdom of those who have gone before us—through times no less uncertain, yet just as full of potential.

Your Turn

As we close this chapter, now's the time to pause, reflect, and begin putting some of these ideas into practice. These questions and exercises are designed to help you deepen your creative identity, sharpen your voice, and begin cultivating the kind of originality no machine can touch.

Questions

1 In what ways might you be unconsciously allowing formulaic, predictable patterns to shape your creative work? Where could you intentionally break from those habits and explore new, unfamiliar territory?

2 How might your creative process shift if you focused less on producing answers and more on asking better, more interesting questions?

3 How might embracing this season of disruption lead you to rethink not just your art, but how you share it, distribute it, or connect it to an audience?

Exercises

1 Write a Letter from Future You to Present You:
Imagine yourself ten years from now. What kind of creative life are you living? What steps did you take to get there? What kinds of risks did you take? What words of encouragement would you share?

2 Reverse Engineering Exercise:
Pick an influential piece of art from the past that thrived because it broke from tradition during a disruptive time. Analyze what made it radical *then*, and brainstorm how you might apply a similar spirit of reinvention to your own medium *now*.

3 The Alien Critic:
Imagine a being who has never seen human creativity before is looking, hearing, or tasting your latest work. What would the alien see, hear, or taste that you can't? What might it find strange, repetitive, beautiful, or boring? What about your piece would make them care about it? Sometimes, stepping outside our own lens can help us see where our originality actually lives.

Notes

1 Schneider, Pierre. *The World of Manet, 1832–1883.* Time Life Books, 1968.

2 Eccl 1:9 (NIV).

3 Aurelius, Marcus. *Meditations.* Translated by Gregory Hays. Modern Library, 2002.

4 Tolle, Eckhart. *The Power of Now: A Guide to Spiritual Enlightenment.* New World Library, 1999.

5 Eves, Howard. *Return to Mathematical Circles: A Fifth Collection of Mathematical Stories and Anecdotes.* PWS-Kent Publishing Company, 1988.

6 Fisher, Mark. *Ghosts of My Life: Writings on Depression, Hauntology and Lost Futures.* Zero Books, 2014.

7 Michaels, Sean. "Pop Music These Days: It All Sounds the Same, Survey Reveals." *The Guardian*, July 27, 2012. Accessed December 15, 2025. https://www.theguardian.com/music/2012/jul/27/pop-music-sounds-same-survey-reveals.

8 Barnes, Tom. "Scientists Just Discovered Why All Pop Music Sounds Exactly the Same." *Mic*, January 7, 2015. Accessed December 15, 2025. https://www.mic.com/articles/107896/scientists-finally-prove-why-pop-music-all-sounds-the-same.

9 Hume, Billy. "The Real Reason Why Today's Music Is Starting to Sound the Same." *Freaking Out with Billy Hume*, November 8, 2024. https://www.youtube.com/watch?v=JZgPKGVJrdc.

10 Mastroianni, Adam. "Pop Culture Has Become an Olihopoly." *Experimental History*, May 2, 2022. Accessed December 15, 2025. https://www.experimental-history.com/p/pop-culture-has-become-an-oligopoly.

11 Fisher, Mark. *Ghosts of My Life: Writings on Depression, Hauntology and Lost Futures.* Zero Books, 2014.

12 Barkan, Ross. "The Rise of the New Romanticism." *Political Currents by Ross Barkan*, November 29, 2024. Accessed December 15, 2025. https://rosselliotbarkan.com/p/the-rise-of-the-new-romanticism.

13 Gioia, Ted. "Are We Living in a Time of Cultural Collapse?" *The Honest Broker*, May 7, 2025. Accessed December 15, 2025. https://www.honest-broker.com/p/are-we-living-in-a-time-of-cultural.

14 Video Game Insights. *Global Indie Games Market Report 2024*. October 2024. Accessed December 15, 2025. https://vginsights.com/assets/reports/VGI_Global_Indie_Games_Market_Report_2024.pdf.

15 Godin, Seth. *Purple Cow: Transform Your Business by Being Remarkable*. Portfolio, 2003.

16 Baudelaire, Charles. *The Mirror of Art: Critical Studies*. Translated and edited by Jonathan Mayne. Doubleday Anchor Books, 1956.

Part II

Reclaiming Creative Power

How We Move Forward

6 Using the Tools Without Becoming One

All significant breakthroughs are break-"withs" old ways of thinking.[1]

SCIENTIFIC AUTHOR THOMAS KUHN

Recording drums is hard. In short, you need a great drummer playing a great kit in a great room, recorded with great microphones. All of that equals a great sound. If any link in that chain is weak, you're going to struggle when it comes time to mix.

Nowadays, if an artist doesn't have much of a budget to record real drums in a proper studio, there's no shortage of software options. But back in 1979, that just wasn't possible. There were a few basic drum machines, but you were stuck with whatever patterns were programmed at the factory, and the sounds were absolutely dreadful, limited to generic beeps and boops. Frustrated by those constraints, guitarist Roger Linn decided there had to be a better way. After talking it over with his friend, Toto keyboardist Steve Porcaro, Linn made a bold decision: he would build his own.

By the late 1970s, computer technology had finally become affordable enough to store "samples" on a mid-sized machine. In practical terms, this meant Roger could capture short recordings of a real drummer hitting a real drum and have that play back as the sounds. When he paired that idea with a simple sequencer that allowed users to arrange those samples into any rhythm they wanted, he realized he had hit on something revolutionary. It didn't take long for his prototype to get noticed.

Linn first showed his invention to the singer-songwriter Leon Russell, who often relied on drum machines to make demos. Russell was immediately impressed and asked to buy one. He went on to use it for the final drum parts on every track of his 1979 album *Life and Love*. Quickly after, other musical acts and recording studios were dying to buy one. For a young twenty-something guitarist like Linn, his little invention became a hit beyond his wildest dreams.

The LM-1 debuted in 1980 as the first product from Linn Electronics. Promising "real drums at your fingertips,"[2] the LM-1 helped establish drum machines as "credible, powerful instruments,"[3] rather than toys. Its sampled sounds quickly became part of the soundtrack of the 1980s, appearing on blockbuster hits by artists like Prince, Queen, and Michael Jackson. Unfortunately, as Linn's drum machine began rising in popularity, many professional drummers began fretting about their future.

This concern was not unfounded. After all, the machines didn't tire, didn't need breaks, and didn't ask for royalties. With the clarity of hindsight, we know the end of the story: drummers didn't go extinct. But at the time, many blamed Roger and his company for pop culture's obsession with this new sound. Out of defense, Linn stated:

> It really is a drummer's tool. It's just become part of their kit and . . . they can do things they couldn't do on a kit anyway. It's also true that when someone who isn't a drummer programs the machine on a record, it sounds like it. It sounds very repetitive, dull and lifeless, and when a real drummer uses his creativity to program a drum machine and all the nuances of the song he'd play anyway, then the song sounds much more creative, and the drums really respond to the music.[4]

He wasn't wrong. Just like a drummer carrying a shaker or tambourine, drum machines have become part of most drummers' toolkit. They offer a *different* sound, but in no way better. Besides, even if a record was recorded entirely with a drum machine (like Russell's *Life and Love*), no one would have wanted to go out on tour with a small, black box substituting for a real drummer pounding out the groove. Like hi-hats and toms, drum machines just became another extension of the creative drummer.

As new models and manufacturers entered the market, these devices began to spawn entirely new genres like house, techno, and industrial. Most of the drummers who came out on top proved to be those who were willing to adapt. They learned when to play their acoustic kits, when to set down their sticks for sequencers, and when to blend live rhythm with electronic pulse, pivoting whenever the genre demanded.

Perhaps these drummers should have felt guilty about adopting the drum machine. After all, there were undeniably some who lost work from sessions that didn't require a real person. These musicians could have likely been seen as traitors to the profession. But in the end, the machines didn't replace drummers; they simply redefined what drummers could do. They expanded the vocabulary of rhythm and empowered players to become architects of a completely different sound.

Fifty Shades of Data

It might seem strange to encounter a chapter on potentially utilizing generative AI, when I've spent so much time championing the undisputed roar of human creativity. While I am fully convinced that AI will *never* replace the human artist, I also believe that it could serve as a helpful, albeit flawed, tool in the artist's toolbox. This is, undeniably, a fine line to walk as there are legitimate concerns about the origins and ongoing development of generative AI—some of which we've already explored. But to not include a chapter on how one might choose to integrate this technology into their work would be naïve, shortsighted, and disingenuous. The distinction, as I see it, lies not so much in whether we engage with AI, but *how*.

The truth here is that, like social media or any other ethically compromised technology, the decision of if, when, and how to utilize AI is a deeply personal one, based off one's own convictions and conscience. What feels ethically neutral to one person may strike another as deeply troubling. Where the line gets drawn is likely not going to be purely black or white, but somewhere in the gray.

Acknowledging complexity isn't to deflect moral responsibility; it's how we meet it honestly. AI is here and, like it or not, millions of people are already using it in both interesting and troubling ways. Some will reject the technology outright, and they should have that right. For those of us who see potential though, the task is to walk a narrow line of embracing curiosity without surrendering discernment.

What I believe ultimately matters, is that if we choose to engage, we do so ethically, refusing the luxury of ignorance. That begins by pausing long enough to reflect upon the implications of implementation. This needn't be an abstract or academic inquiry; it's a moral checkpoint for people living in an age where innovation often outpaces introspection.

The modern world is, to put it mildly, complicated. For many families living on a tight budget, buying bargain clothes from big box retailers or questionable online marketplaces can feel like the only practical choice. Yet these low prices often come with the hidden costs of environmental harm, exploitative labor practices, and ethically compromised supply chains. Similarly, everyday tasks such as purchasing a tomato at your nearby supermarket, choosing to listen to music on a particular streaming platform, or replacing an old TV can have ramifications that transcend far beyond your own life. In his book *The Longing for Less*, author Kyle Chayka reminds us:

> We might be able to hold the iPhone in our hands, but we should also be aware that the network of its consequences is vast: server farms absorbing massive amounts of electricity, Chinese factories where workers die by suicide, devastated mud pit mines that produce tin. It's easy to feel like a minimalist when you can order food, summon a car, or rent a room using a single brick of steel and silicon. But in reality it's the opposite. We're taking advantage of a maximalist assemblage. Just because something looks simple doesn't mean it is; the aesthetics of simplicity cloak artifice or even unsustainable excess.[5]

Most choices that we make carry economic, environmental, and cultural ripple effects. We rarely see those effects in real time, which makes it easy to forget they exist. But whether we're talking about global supply chains or digital infrastructures, every convenience comes with a cost, often paid by someone, somewhere, out of sight. The same principle applies to creativity. Understanding those ripples, and acting within them thoughtfully, is what distinguishes ethical creation from naïve participation.

While there are many things to consider as you contemplate if, when, and how you utilize specific AI systems, three areas of impact deserve particular attention:

- The Environment,
- Ethical Training, and
- Labor Conditions.

The Environment

When Beverly and Jeff Morris bought their dream home in rural Mansfield, Georgia, they never imagined that within a few years, Meta would be building a massive data center less than 400 yards from their property. Built to power AI and cloud computing, the facility replaced the once quiet, nearby forest with dust, light pollution, and constant industrial noise. Not long after construction began, the Morrises noticed murky sediment in their well water and a sharp drop in water pressure. The contamination damaged their plumbing and appliances, forcing them to store bottled water just to flush toilets. Soon after, their monthly power bill jumped from around $250 a month to over $400.[6]

Their story is emblematic of a larger issue: while companies like Meta profit from the explosive demands of cloud computing, nearby residents bear the environmental and economic costs. Many communities also report health effects from the perpetual hum of data centers. Sleep disorders, headaches, anxiety, and cardiovascular stress have been to be statistically higher in these areas.[7] Even wildlife suffers, as constant mechanical noise disrupts migration and breeding patterns.

Scientists estimate that power consumption of North American data centers swelled from 2,688 megawatts in 2022 to 5,341 megawatts in 2023, driven largely by AI's computation hunger. By 2026, the global electrical consumption of data centers is expected to approach 1,050 terawatt-hours.[8] As a point of comparison, this is roughly equivalent to the entire nation of Japan.[9] Similarly, researchers at Cornell University project that by 2027, AI operations could consume up to 6.6 billion cubic meters of fresh water annually.[10] This is roughly *half* of all of the UK's annual usage.

Entire books have been written on the environmental toll of large data centers and AI infrastructure. My goal here isn't to catalog every harm, but to stress the reality that technology carries ethical weight. The world's resources are finite, and every generation has a duty to steward them wisely. As we integrate AI into our workflows, we would do well to ensure that our pursuit of innovation doesn't eclipse our duty to sustainability. True progress keeps both our craft and our planet in view.

Ethical Training

On July 16, 2025, bestselling novelist David Baldacci testified before the U.S. Senate Judiciary Subcommittee on Crime and Counterterrorism during a hearing titled "Too Big to Prosecute?: Examining the AI Industry's Mass Ingestion of Copyrighted Works for AI Training." At the hearing, Baldacci described how his son once asked ChatGPT to write a plot "in the style of a David Baldacci novel." The system produced characters, twists, and scenes drawn directly from several of his books. "It felt," he said, "as if someone had backed up a truck to my imagination and stolen everything I'd ever created."

Baldacci rejected the notion that AI "learns" like a writer. Instead, he argued, these systems are trained on full, often pirated copies of authors' works. He called it "the largest criminal-level copyright infringement ever perpetrated in this country," warning that AI-generated knockoffs now appear alongside legitimate books, siphoning sales, confusing readers, and eroding the value of original work. His recommendations to Congress were clear: empower authors to block access to pirated datasets, require transparency in AI training materials, and mandate labeling for AI-generated content.

While Baldacci stood before Congress primarily as an author, his testimony served as both a witness and a representative of countless creatives. Unfortunately, most major AI models are currently built on a foundation of intellectual property that was scraped, sorted, and synthesized without consent. Machines cannot train themselves. If they're to sound, look, and act human, they need to be trained on human creativity and, well, as the expression goes: "why pay for the cow if you can get the milk for free?"

When *The Wall Street Journal* interviewed OpenAI's former CTO, Mira Murati, about their then-upcoming video generation model, Sora, her evasiveness spoke volumes. When asked where OpenAI sourced all of its training data, Murati replied vaguely: "We used publicly available data and licensed data." When the interviewer shot back, "so . . . videos from YouTube?" Murati paused, looked confused, and shot back: "mmm, I'm actually not sure."

Now, remember, this is the company's *Chief Technology Officer*.

When the interviewer again pressed about data sourcing, this time asking if they used people's Facebook and Instagram videos, Murati again fumbled:

"I'm not sure. I'm not confident about it." Finally, asked whether the company used material from Shutterstock—a company that OpenAI is in partnership with—Murati concluded, "I'm just not going to go into the details of the data that was used."[11]

Contrast this to only one year later, when OpenAI released their Sora 2 app and dropped any illusion of avoiding copyrighted material. Even amid litigation from companies such as Disney, Universal, and Warner Bros, prompts requesting videos to be generated of SpongeBob, James Bond, Mickey Mouse, or Mario were generated without hesitation. Although the wave of blatant rip-offs on the platform was short-lived, the audacity of permitting them at all revealed a striking shift in OpenAI's public messaging. What once required denial suddenly became justifiable appropriation (interestingly, within three months, OpenAI and Disney reached a licensing agreement, clearly acknowledging a need for credit, consent, and compensation for IP holders).

Caring about the integrity of our work means remaining attentive to the moral complexities that surround it. Though the modern world is endlessly complicated, we must resist surrendering our moral judgment to claims of technological inevitability. As we pull back the curtain on the unseen human cost behind AI, it should become clear that the question isn't just *what* these systems are built from, but *who* they're built upon, and who they may continue to affect.

Labor Conditions

When you think of the world of those developing AI, what image do you see? If you're anything like me, you probably see data scientists working in posh Silicon Valley workspaces. What many of us don't realize though is that around 80 percent of the time spent on training AI consists of labeling datasets.

"Humans in the loop" (or HITL) are known as those who are responsible for sorting, labeling, and sifting through vast oceans of online content, often for as little as $1.50 an hour in countries like Kenya, India, the Philippines, and Venezuela. Their work exists because AI systems cannot reliably perceive moral or emotional nuance without human judgment. Machines can recognize patterns, but they don't understand context (e.g., satire versus hate, documentation versus exploitation).

Unfortunately, much of what these workers are asked to view is horrific. In 2024, *CBS News* interviewed Naftali Wambalo, a Kenyan father of two with a mathematics degree, who shared: "I looked at people being slaughtered. People engaging in sexual activity with animals. People abusing children physically, sexually. People committing suicide."[12] Wambalo is now 1 of 200 workers suing Meta and others for "unreasonable working conditions" that caused severe psychological trauma.

Many tech companies do whatever they can to obscure the human cost of their so-called automation. As Oxford Professors Drs. James Muldoon, Mark Graham, and Callum Cant write in *Feeding the Machine: The Hidden Human Labour Powering AI*:

> By using AI products we are directly inserting ourselves into the lives of workers dispersed across the globe. We are connected whether we like it or not. Just as drinking a cup of coffee implicates the coffee drinker in a global production network from bean to cup, we should all understand how using a search engine, a chatbot—or even something as simple as a smart robot vacuum—sets in motion global flows of data and capital that connect workers, organisations and consumers in every corner of the planet.[13]

The irony is that the very systems designed to automate certain aspects of human labor still completely depend on it. If we're to call ourselves principled creators, we must recognize that "artificial" intelligence is anything but; it runs on real people, with real costs.

An Ethical Framework

After reading all of this, you might be thinking, "Well, if that's what goes into creating and running the major AI systems, there's no way I'm going to find ethically pure options." Sadly, you may be right. While some systems are certainly less compromised than others, I'm doubtful that any of the dominant solutions can currently be considered "100% guilt-free." Organizations such as Fairly Trained (www.fairlytrained.org) can serve as

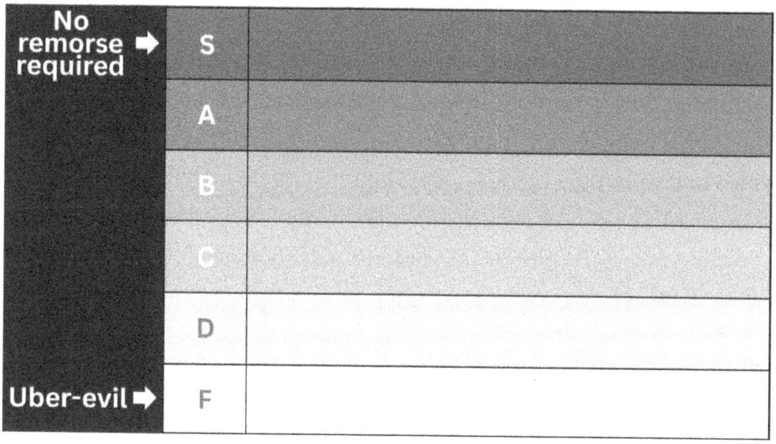

Figure 6.1 *An ethical tier list.*

helpful starting points for assessing options, but as we've seen, there's more to things than just training.

That's precisely why, at the start of this chapter, I emphasized that the decision of if, when, and how you integrate AI into your creative process is a deeply personal one. So, how do we evaluate the AI tools we might consider engaging? Are there any frameworks that can help us choose technologies that serve both our craft and our conscience?

If you've spent any time on YouTube, you've likely seen videos that rank everything from snack foods to video games. Admittedly, I'm a sucker for these kinds of videos. Most creators make these by incorporating a popular, universal template known as the *YouTube Tier List*. Basically, it's a chart that places the "best" at the top under the S-tier (for "superior"), followed by A, B, C, D, and F-tiers. As I've undergone my own ethics audit on various AI tools, I have found this kind of visual ranking surprisingly helpful.

For example, in our version, let's say that the F-tier represents the *worst* of AI—examples that clearly hurt people, the environment, and the shared social contract. Meanwhile, the S-tier will represent the least harmful or even globally beneficial uses. Such a list might look something like what is shown in Figure 6.1.

As you develop your own ethical tier list, questions like these can help you assess systems before you integrate them into your work:

1 Purpose: "How and why am I using it?"
Consider the context in which you're turning to AI. Are you seeking efficiency, experimentation, or evasion? To me, there's a world of difference between employing it as a brainstorming partner—generating ideas, expanding your palette, or shaping an outline—versus letting it function as the primary generator of a finished piece. One feels like helpful assistance; the other feels more like pressing a button on a vending machine and then taking credit for making the bag of chips that drops out.

Example: Using an AI video tool to generate placeholder shots for a project-in-development might fall into your C-tier. But relying on it to quickly churn out AI slop in hopes of jumpstarting a YouTube side hustle might be better off in the F-tler.

2. Prevalence: "How often am I relying on it?"
Understanding AI's footprint is important, yet reliable data on the energy and environmental costs of AI inference (the stage where trained models generate new outputs) is currently quite limited. Occasional use of text-based AI tends to consume minimal resources, while habitual dependence on image, video, or audio generators can quickly compound impact.[14] Furthermore, occasional use of AI in your creative work may be helpful for inspiration or iteration, but an over-reliance can quickly dilute your unique voice. Be mindful of how often you turn to these tools and ask whether it's helping you deepen your craft or merely empowering laziness.

Example: A designer using a fully licensed image generator a few times a week to lay out concept ideas might land in their S-tier. But generating hundreds of images daily, rapidly iterating on slight variations, would quickly slide much further down the scale.

3. Impact: "Who or what is affected by my use of it?"
As the authors of *Feeding the Machine* rightly pointed out, technology tends to have an economic, environmental, and human ripple effect. Consider how your use of AI might affect others. Does it uplift others or undercut them? Awareness of impact transforms private decisions into public responsibility.

Example: A songwriter might consider using a voice-changing AI tool from a company listed on www.fairlytrained.org to fall into their B-tier—a practical and ethically sourced extension of their craft. But releasing a track that uses an unlicensed model trained on a non-consenting artist's voice might land at the very bottom of their list.

You won't always find neat answers. Some tools may feel ethically neutral, others clearly problematic, and many will live somewhere in-between. The point is to engage thoughtfully, to pause before you act, and to make choices that align with both your artistic vision and your moral compass. You don't have to have all the answers, but practicing discernment can preserve your humanity as you consider if, when, and how to integrate AI into your work.

Three Paths to the Canvas

In this wild, wild west where human and synthetic content compete for attention, influence, and income, it's worth taking a closer look at the evolving landscape of creative production. The way I see it, today's creative processes generally fall into three distinct categories:

- Human-generated,
- AI-generated, and
- Human-generated, AI-assisted.

To encourage thoughtful exploration, I want to unpack each category and offer some interesting, modern examples that illustrate how today's creative process is diversifying.

The first variation, human-generated, should be self-explanatory. It's the mode of creativity that has always existed with humans completely at the helm, drawing from their lived experiences, identity, intuition, and imagination. This form of creativity remains the benchmark against which all other forms are measured.

The second category, AI-generated, is where the output is fully shaped by artificial intelligence. A human may provide the initial prompt or direction, but the final product is synthesized by the machine. This approach can be valuable for experimentation or rapid prototyping, but it also undoubtedly raises many of the ethical, philosophical, and qualitative issues we've been exploring. Instead of rehashing those concerns, I want to highlight a few lesser-discussed aspects of this category.

First, while many of today's generative AI platforms are unfairly scraping and repurposing the intellectual property of countless creatives, there are emerging models that aim to do things differently. Systems like Infinity Album (https://www.infinitealbum.io/) and Jen (https://www.jenmusic.ai/) are experimenting with frameworks that compensate artists, give proper credit, and operate with consent at their core. Rather than being replaced, artists become invaluable to these systems, licensing previous work into them.[15]

Second, some artists are using proprietary AI systems to create entirely new forms of art. Take Refik Anadol: his commissioned piece, *Unsupervised*, continuously reimagines and mutates artworks from the Museum of Modern Art's collection into an unending, never-repeating flow of color and motion. It's a mesmerizing, evolving, and legally licensed portrait of human creativity as interpreted by a machine. Anadol was also the first artist to utilize the Exosphere at the Sphere in Las Vegas, using real-time weather data from nearby sensors tracking wind, precipitation, and air pressure to influence the visuals onscreen. Works like this show how chance, automation, and consensually used data can merge to produce new art forms that blur the line between human and machine.

Last on the list is the category that is likely to intersect with the majority of creatives: human-generated, AI-assisted. In this variation, humans remain central to the creative act, but use AI tools to enhance, refine, or accelerate their work. For example, a photographer might take a real photo and then use AI to remove unwanted objects in the background. Most modern smartphones have been offering this sort of tech-assisted capability for years.

Nearly every creative field is experiencing a wave of AI-powered tools. Architects, for instance, now have access to platforms like Autodesk Forma, which uses AI to analyze site conditions (e.g., sun, wind, noise) and generate optimal massing and layout options. This can be helpful for early-stage planning and feasibility studies. Likewise, many fashion designers are using platforms like CLO 3D and Browzwear to simulate garment draping, fit, and movement. These apps can reduce the need for physical samples and speed up prototyping.

In film and video production, some editors are using AI to automate tasks like color correction, scene detection, and even rough cuts. Adobe Premiere Pro now includes AI features that can match color grades across shots or remove filler words from dialogue with a single click. Used correctly, none of these tools should replace creatives' sensibilities, but allow for a shorter distance between having a technical problem and solving it.

Personally, I've found certain AI tools to be incredibly helpful to my creative process. As a music producer, I often face budgets that require me to wear multiple hats: arranging, recording, mixing, and mastering. Mixing involves shaping individual tracks like vocals, drums, and guitars into a cohesive stereo mix. Mastering is the final step, preparing that mix for release and ensuring it sounds consistent across playback systems, from earbuds to car speakers.

While I love mixing, I'm often reluctant to master my own mixes. It's a highly technical process that, at least for me, is hard to objectify after you've lived so long with your own mix. It's like trying to edit a novel you've read a hundred times—you start to lose perspective. That's why I will often use an AI-assisted mastering tool (e.g., iZotope's Ozone) to preview how a finished track might sound. I rarely keep the AI-assisted master, but using it as a reference gives me a target to surpass with my own tools. This approach allows me to benefit from AI's "outside view" without surrendering my creative judgment to it.

As an educator, I've taken a similar approach with my songwriting students, giving them permission to utilize an LLM as a lyrical brainstorming partner. Not because it writes great lyrics. God, no. Most of what it spits out lacks any emotional depth or creative brilliance (more on this in the next chapter). Still, it can be useful for generating ideas around a theme or summarizing storytelling concepts into concise pathways. Ultimately, I leave this decision up to my students.

I can already hear the detractors: "Why would you let your students cheat?" "Why allow them to use systems that cause such societal harm?" While I empathize with these questions, I'm also realistic. Students know this technology exists, and most are already using it in various parts of their lives. The data clearly shows this.[16]

Large scale adoption is happening within the creative community as well. In late 2025, Adobe partnered with The Harris Poll to survey over 16,000 emerging content creators across the globe.[17] They reported that 86 percent of respondents said they now actively integrate generative AI into their workflows with the most common uses being editing, upscaling, and enhancement (55 percent), and brainstorming and ideation (48 percent). But even as adoption surged, 69 percent expressed unease about their content being used to train AI without permission, making it one of the top barriers to further adoption.

This data paints a picture of a creative community that's both intrigued and unsettled—and is exactly why I'd rather lead by teaching the pros and cons, empowering students and artistic colleagues to decide if, when, and how to employ it. If I'm doing my job well, I'm not forcing my own views on them. I'm helping them think critically and use their own minds to discern and create.

AI-assistance needn't be a taboo topic we whisper about in hallways. We need to talk about it, openly and often, so we can think clearly about what it means to adopt, if/when it makes sense, and how to do it responsibly.

The Creative Response

Technological leaps always trigger disruption. From the invention of photography to the rise of sampling in music, new tools have always challenged the status quo. But amid that tension, artists have consistently found ways to adapt, evolve, and flourish.

While advocating for what's right, we as artists must resist the pull of fear and instead cultivate a learner's mindset. Just as the drum machines of the 1980s once upset traditional beat-making—ultimately unlocking new genres and creative possibilities—some of today's AI resources may hold similar potential, serving as invitations to rethink how we approach our canvas.

With a framework rooted in ethical exploration, curiosity can be a powerful conduit for inspiration, experimentation, and ingenuity. In his book *The Creative Act*, music producer Rick Rubin rightly states, "The world is constantly changing, so no matter how often we practice paying attention, there will always be something new to notice. It's up to us to find it."[18] That's the challenge and the gift of being a creative in this moment.

What all this disruption means for you and your work will always remain a uniquely personal thing. Regardless of where you land, in this time where imitation is effortless, perhaps one of the hardest tasks will be moving forward with clarity, conviction, and a voice that remains unmistakably your own. Not because you necessarily resist change, but because you know how to meet it without losing yourself.

Your Turn

As we close this chapter, now's the time to pause, reflect, and begin putting some of these ideas into practice. These questions and exercises are designed to help you deepen your creative identity, sharpen your voice, and begin cultivating the kind of originality no machine can touch.

Questions

1 How did this chapter resonate with you? How comfortable are you with creating work that's AI-assisted?

2 If you were to integrate some version of AI into your creative practice, what role would it play? How might it expand, or limit, your artistic vision?

3 Where do you draw the line between using (any form of) technology as a creative partner and letting it take the wheel? What boundaries might you need to draw so that you remain the one steering your creative process?

Exercises

1 Your Own Ethical Tier List:

Create your own tier list, ranking the creative tools you use. Reflect on where your ethical comfort zone lies, and what that might say about your work.

2 Trace the Chain:

Pick one digital tool you use often—a plug-in, platform, or program. Research where it comes from: who built it, how it's trained, and what it might cost the world to run.

3 Creative Blindfold:

For one project, intentionally remove one sense, one tool, or one comfort. Write a song without instruments. Paint without sight. Design with paper and glue. Let constraint reveal what your intuition remembers.

Notes

1 Kuhn, Thomas S. *The Structure of Scientific Revolutions*. University of Chicago Press, 1962.

2 McNamee, David. "Linn and Oberheim Drum Machines." *The Guardian*, June 22, 2009. Accessed December 15, 2025. https://www.theguardian.com/music/2009/jun/22/linn-oberheim-drum-machines.

3 Ibid.

4 Horkins, Tony. "I Murdered the Drummer." *International Musician & Recording World*, June 1985. Accessed December 15, 2025. https://www.muzines.co.uk/articles/i-murdered-the-drummer/12513.

5 Chayka, Kyle. *The Longing for Less: Living with Minimalism*. Bloomsbury Publishing, 2020.

6 More Perfect Union. "I Live 400 Yards from Mark Zuckerberg's Massive Data Center." *YouTube video*, March 27, 2025. Accessed December 15, 2025. https://www.youtube.com/watch?v=DGjj7wDYail&t=123s.

7 Fairfax Station Connection. "Residents Speak Out Against Data Center." *Fairfax Station Connection*, September 27, 2023. Accessed December 15, 2025. https://www.fairfaxstationconnection.com/news/2023/sep/27/residents-speak-out-against-data-center/.

8 Zewe, Adam. "Explained: Generative AI's Environmental Impact." *MIT News*, January 17, 2025. Accessed December 15, 2025. https://news.mit.edu/2025/explained-generative-ai-environmental-impact-0117.

9 To be fair, the rollout of generative AI also appears to be accelerating the deployment and optimization of cleaner energy systems. With the growing demand that AI is placing on existing power grids, many companies and communities are rising to meet that demand by aligning AI infrastructure with clean energy transitions.

10 Li, Pengfei, Yang, Jianyi, Islam, Mohammad A., and Ren, Shaolei. "Making AI Less 'Thirsty': Uncovering and Addressing the Secret Water Footprint of AI Models." *arXiv*, April 2023. Accessed December 15, 2025. https://arxiv.org/abs/2304.03271.

11 Stern, Joanna. "OpenAI CTO on the Future of Sora, ChatGPT, and AI Rivals: Full Interview." *Wall Street Journal Video*, April 11, 2024. Accessed December 15, 2025. https://www.wsj.com/video/series/joanna-stern-personal

-technology/openai-cto-on-the-future-of-sora-chatgpt-and-ai-rivals-full-interview/C7D3FD48-5A1C-41A0-B5F4-B939AF357458.

12 Stahl, Lesley, Chasan, Aliza, Bar-On, Shachar, and Jung, Jinsol. "Kenyan Workers with AI Jobs Thought They Had Tickets to the Future Until the Grim Reality Set In." *CBS News*, November 24, 2024. Accessed December 15, 2025. https://www.cbsnews.com/news/ai-work-kenya-exploitation-60-minutes/.

13 Muldoon, James, Graham, Mark, and Cant, Callum. *Feeding the Machine: The Hidden Human Labour Powering AI*. Canongate, 2024.

14 According to a 2025 Cornell University study, the inference of most LLMs averages somewhere between 0.42 and 33 watt-hours per query. This number fluctuates wildly depending on the model being used and the complexity of the query. This study can be found at https://arxiv.org/abs/2505.09598.

15 As we explored in Chapter 3, the fight for the artist's three Cs—consent, credit, and compensation—is only going to grow more urgent as these technologies evolve. Without it, tech companies will continue to have carte blanche to pillage and steal from artists in order to build their own empires.

16 Just two months after OpenAI launched ChatGPT, a survey of 1,000 college students found that nearly 90 percent had used the chatbot to help with homework. See https://nymag.com/intelligencer/article/openai-chatgpt-ai-cheating-education-college-students-school.html.

17 Adobe. "Inaugural Adobe Creators' Toolkit Report: 86 Percent of Global Creators Use Creative Generative AI, See It Boosting Creator Economy." *Adobe Newsroom*, October 28, 2025. Accessed December 15, 2025. https://news.adobe.com/news/2025/10/adobe-max-2025-creators-survey.

18 Rubin, Rick and Strauss, Neil. *The Creative Act: A Way of Being*. Penguin Press, 2023.

7 Craft Is the New Creative Currency

Inspiration exists, but it has to find us working.[1]

PABLO PICASSO

In June 2021, GitHub (a platform that allows developers to create, store, and share their code) released its generative AI assistant, Copilot, as a technical preview. Marketed as a game-changing tool that could write code for apps, websites, and software, the pitch was wildly seductive: Instead of hiring expensive engineers or slogging through countless hours of debugging, why not let AI do it all? Type a prompt, get instant code, move on. But when a group of cybersecurity researchers from New York University put Copilot to the test, the results were a shadow of what was promised.

The team created eighty-nine scenarios for Copilot to generate code, resulting in 1,692 programs. An independent audit later revealed that nearly 40 percent of the generated programs contained serious bugs or design flaws that could easily be exploited by novice hackers.[2] These problems were open doors that hackers would have walked through countless times before—vulnerabilities so obvious that even mid-level programmers would have known to avoid them. You see, programming, like any creative field, evolves. Yesterday's inventive solutions eventually become today's stale clichés.[3]

Like all other forms of generative AI, Copilot builds on recycled patterns, producing code that reflects the average of its training data. In this instance, average meant insecure. Beyond programming though, this case serves as a prime example of AI's shortcomings in any creative discipline. When machines are trained on what is most common, they excel at producing what is fast, cheap, and well-worn. What these systems consistently fail to grasp are the pivotal distinctions that elevate artistic work from "good enough" to "great:" the subtleties, exceptions, and leaps of thought that simply cannot be reduced to an algorithm.

The Fast, Cheap, and Great Paradox

One of the greatest tensions facing artists today is the reality that we live in a culture that tends to prize voluminous output. We want everything *now*. This kind of mentality is possible in our Temu, AliExpress, and IKEA-obsessed culture. When fast and cheap are the top priorities though, there's just one problem: greatness becomes the casualty.

Early on in my creative career, I learned this axiom the hard way. It's one I've seen play out thousands of times in every sector of the marketplace.

Examine each of the intersections: if something must be fast and cheap, it will inevitably result in low quality. If something must be cheap and great, it typically takes a great deal of time. The paradox is that you can only pick two; all three factors cannot coexist. Anyone claiming otherwise is selling snake oil—or, as my grandmother-in-law used to say, "full of blue mud."

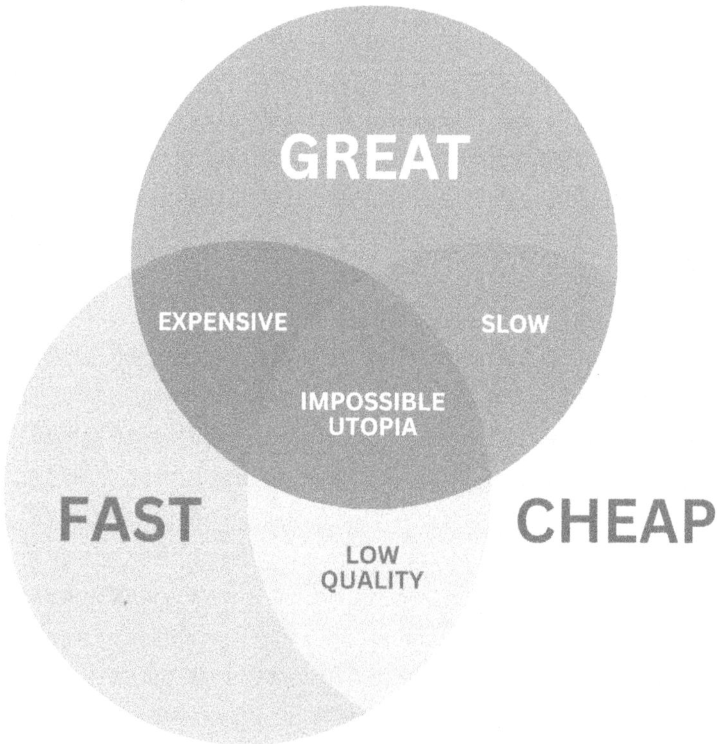

Figure 7.1 *The fast, cheap, and great paradox.*

To demonstrate, let's take a look at the world of fast fashion. At its core, this business model takes the latest runway trends, mass-produces them at breakneck speed, and floods the market while demand is at its peak. Brands like Shein, Zara, and H&M have built empires on this approach, promising the newest styles for next to nothing. But the low-price tag carries different costs that don't show up on the receipt.

The fabrics are often made from synthetic materials, chemical-laden, and hazardous. Stitching frays, hems unravel, and garments lose their shape after only a few washes. Fit is an afterthought; most pieces are cut for "one-size-fits-most" efficiency, which really translates to "one-size-that-fits-no-one." Behind the clothes is a world of dimly lit rooms, relentless shifts, and wages so low they barely cover a meal. Razor thin margins mean that even the "good" jobs demand laborers work 75–80 hour weeks just to earn a livable wage. Meanwhile, much of the cotton is sourced from farms where forced labor—slavery by another name—is disturbingly common.

Fast and cheap? Absolutely.
Fast, cheap, and *great*? Not a chance.

The confluence of AI and the arts is no different. In a race for efficiency and price, artificial intelligence will almost always outpace humanity. But potently poignant work simply does not come immediate and discounted. The beauty of it is part of its limitation—the time it took, the scars it carries, the price it cost. There's just something unmistakable about work that comes from a place of deep attention.

In a time when we're pushed to post, publish, and produce on an accelerating loop, there will always be something radical about slowing down. This isn't an excuse for laziness. Art has never been a place where the indolent thrive. No, I'm talking about resisting the pressure to churn and instead, returning to the workbench, carving, sanding, and polishing ideas into something unmistakably great.

This can't happen through constant output. It only happens by sitting with an idea, wrestling with meaning, and waiting for the right note or revising the draft until it breathes. That kind of care is slow and thoughtful. And in the age of AI, *that* is exactly where your edge lies.

What I'm proposing here is to forget trying to beat the machine at its own game. I mean to play a different game entirely. One that only humanity can play, where craft becomes the new currency. When average solutions become fast and cheap, excellence becomes the new scarcity. And scarcity, as always, is where value sits.

Quality Over Quantity

When Hayao Miyazaki, Isao Takahata, and Toshio Suzuki founded Studio Ghibli in 1985, most of Japan's animation industry was anchored to crushing deadlines and shoestring budgets. The goal of most TV series was merely to fill airtime, not to impress, inspire, or evoke. Against that backdrop, Ghibli set out with a different ambition. From its very beginning, the studio defined itself not by how much it produced, but by how beautifully it crafted. Its debut film, *Laputa: Castle in the Sky*, was a statement of intent: breathtakingly hand-drawn worlds, expansive storytelling, and a commitment to treating animation as cinema rather than content.

This choice to move slowly, aiming for excellence rather than efficiency, has come to define the studio's legacy. In nearly forty years, Studio Ghibli has released fewer than twenty-five films. Compared to the conveyor belt of Hollywood animation, this output is minuscule. And yet, this scarcity has only heightened the impact of each new release. A Ghibli film is never "just another" movie; it's an event.

But scarcity without substance wouldn't be enough. What truly makes Ghibli extraordinary is the uncompromising pursuit of excellence. Miyazaki is famous for his perfectionism. During the production of *Princess Mononoke*, he personally redrew or corrected thousands of frames. For *Spirited Away*, he oversaw every detail of the storyboards, ensuring that every shot carried emotional resonance as well as visual splendor. At a time when most animation studios had transitioned to computer graphics, Ghibli clung to the painstaking process of hand-drawing its films, insisting that the time and labor were worth it.

The results vindicated their philosophy. In 1992, their film *Porco Rosso* beat out Disney's *Beauty and the Beast* at the Japanese box office. Then in 2003, *Spirited Away* became the highest-grossing film in Japanese history, pulling in over $200 million before even opening in the US. It was also the first non-English animated film to win an Academy Award.

Their work has not only been embraced by critics, but audiences as well. *Grave of the Fireflies*, *The Tale of the Princess Kaguya*, and *Only Yesterday* all hold a rare and perfect 100 percent rating on Rotten Tomatoes. Eight more of their films all share scores above 90 percent.[4]

The story of Studio Ghibli is, in many ways, a parable for our own cultural moment. We live in an age of abundance, when streaming platforms, franchises, and social media feeds deliver an endless supply of content. The prevailing logic is that more and immediate is better. Ghibli reminds us of the opposite truth: that excellence, particularly when it bears a distinct signature, creates a kind of magic that no flood of fast and cheap can replicate.

From 1986's *Laputa* to 2023's *The Boy and the Heron*, Ghibli's output may be small, but its influence has been enormous. By refusing to bend to the churn of mass production, by choosing artistry over efficiency, Miyazaki and his colleagues built a body of work that has become timeless. In a marketplace obsessed with more, Studio Ghibli has shown the power of less, but better.

If you know where to look, you'll see this philosophical approach in countless other mediums and artists. Miles Davis often retreated for months or even years to experiment with new forms, sounds, and collaborators. He refused to rest on past successes and avoided repeating himself for commercial convenience. Davis prioritized experimentation and quality over sheer volume, ensuring each record pushed musical boundaries.

Similarly, Jonathan Blow is a video game designer who prioritizes conceptual depth and player experience over rapid production. One of his masterpieces, *The Witness*, took seven years to develop, with Blow obsessing over every puzzle and environmental detail. He's publicly criticized the release-games-as-fast-as-possible model, emphasizing that careful iteration and thoughtful design create lasting, meaningful experiences rather than disposable products. In a 2020 podcast interview, Blow stated: "I think we're now in a situation where everybody in the world is flooded with low quality . . . and everybody wishes that they had higher quality."[5]

You don't have to compete in "fast and cheap." In fact, I believe that doing so will not only be highly disadvantageous to you, but perhaps even detrimental to having a sustainable creative career. What will likely play out with generative AI is what has already unfolded in global manufacturing: a trifurcated market where consumers choose between the three realities we've been discussing:

cheap and fast (but subpar), cheap and great (but incredibly slow in a way that benefits the artist), or fast and great (but incredibly expensive in a way that, again, benefits the artist).

We can lament it all we want, but the truth is that AI has cheap and fast locked up. This will certainly mean that many creatives whose work is merely average will struggle. Providing mediocre results in a specialized area (e.g., graphic design, photography, mastering music) used to be just fine when so many people lacked the knowledge or skill set to even attempt it. But AI changes all of that. Now, *everyone* is capable of at least average results.

What AI essentially does is raise the floor of every creative sector. When someone needs something that's merely "good enough," there will likely be no need to hire the human. Artists who want to thrive in this new era will be required to find higher ground.

Ironically, this forced scenario has the potential to be a hidden gift to talented, professional creatives. Before, it was tempting for many of us to believe in the glass ceiling of providing clients and audiences with products that compromised our values. Where we gave away our greatness at breakneck speeds and unsustainable prices. Now, those who truly understand that their greatness has value (i.e., economic scarcity) can reject that pitiful trifecta. In essence, savvy creatives who have confidence in their worth and work have the opportunity to regain the upper hand in the marketplace. They will likely be able to actually charge clients *more money* or *more time*.

Learning from Luxury

As AI accelerates the race to the bottom, we as artists must make the choice to not participate. It's time to stop selling ourselves short by treating higher prices or longer production timelines as negative things. Instead, we should lean into what truly sets us apart—premium experiences and products that unmistakably signal their value. This truism has been at work in countless other industries for ages.

For example, while retailers like Amazon and Walmart will always dominate the cheap-and-fast market, designer houses have carved out an entirely different lane. Unlike fast fashion, luxury brands like Chanel, Burberry, Gucci, Louis Vitton, and Prada all deliberately restrict production, charge much more than necessary, and limit access to their products. They can do this because luxury brands have something most businesses can only dream of: loyal customers who value the brand's greatness over efficiency and cost.

The same principle holds in the automotive world. Consider Ferrari. The average wait time for a new Ferrari is seventeen months. That's by design. Much of the car is still assembled by hand: the stitching of the leather, the crafting of the V12 engine, the countless customization options. That's why a Ferrari ranges from $250,000 to $2.2 million, while a new Ford might cost $30,000. Personalized, handcrafted work has always commanded a premium. The same can be true for your creative endeavors too.

If you doubt this possibility in your own field, I can empathize with your skepticism. Right now, it seems that creatives working within large companies or organizations are particularly vulnerable, as many of these entities are currently choosing cheap and fast over quality. The age of AI has seemed to expose corporate greed more starkly than at any point since the Gilded Age.[6] But in the long run, when this greed reaches a boiling point for paying constituents, they will all see it backfire.

Throughout the first half of the twentieth century, the Milwaukee-based Joseph Schlitz Brewing Company proudly wore the crown as America's largest brewer. Its flagship, Schlitz—"the beer that made Milwaukee famous"—was a beloved and iconic American-style lager.

But in the 1970s, the company made a fateful mistake. Pressured to cut costs and speed up production, executives quietly changed the formula. They replaced malted barley with cheaper corn syrup, shaved down brewing times, and even experimented with adding silica gel to keep the beer looking clear. The accountants were thrilled. The drinkers were not.

Almost overnight, loyal customers noticed something was off. Complaints poured in, sales collapsed, and in 1976 the company was forced into a humiliating recall of 10 million cans and bottles—equivalent to $6.3 million today. By 1981, Schlitz's famous Milwaukee brewery was shuttered. The brand that had once ruled American beer had squandered its crown, and consumers never forgave it.

Historical research consistently shows that most consumers are willing to pay more for quality. Even in a recent study by the Qualtrics XM Institute, three-quarters of respondents said they would gladly spend extra for a premium experience.[7] AI doesn't change this truism; it proves it. Even in its infancy, the rush among CEOs to cut costs with AI is proving to be a fallacy. Customers just aren't putting up with it.

Take the buy-now-pay-later company Klarna. In December 2024, CEO Sebastian Siemiatkowski remarked to Bloomberg that "AI can already do all of the jobs that we, as humans, do."[8] They then slashed 40 percent of their workforce, only to be forced to *rehire* them back after customer backlash.[9] This isn't an outlier; it's the norm.

In January 2024, a survey involving more than 1,400 C-suite executives revealed that 66 percent felt either "ambivalent or outright dissatisfied with their organisation's progress on AI and GenAI so far."[10] Corporate leaders frequently pointed to AI's "lack of talent and skills" as the main problem.[11] Another high-profile study found that more than 55 percent of UK business leaders who substituted human roles with AI now regret that choice (and that's just the leaders who were actually honest with themselves and the study about their disappointment).[12]

If you find yourself working in or for a company that is threatening to outsource roles such as yours to AI, I'm sorry. One of my least favorite things about our current moment is how gleefully most tech company leaders talk about AI replacing jobs. It's cruel, shortsighted, and madly misguided.

A question you might consider asking is if your client or company is one that is trying to win the race to the bottom (i.e., fast and cheap). If so, it may indeed be time to break out the resume. If not, know that this is a marketplace trend that *will* (dare I say must?) correct itself. Price matters of course, but it's not everything. History is replete with companies and organizations that thought they could make shortsighted cuts to the workforce in an effort to slash the bottom line at the customer's expense. But businesses without happy customers quickly become businesses without any customers.

So where does this leave us? If the trifurcated marketplace theory holds true across most disciplines—and I believe it does—then the door is opening for creative craftsmen and women to not just survive, but to perhaps thrive like never before. There's a catch though: the only ones who will be able to capitalize on this will be those who can clearly define *where* and *how* their work is truly excellent.

Business philosophy often emphasizes the importance of a unique selling proposition (USP)—the distinctive benefit or feature that sets a that product, service, or brand apart from its competitors. A strong USP communicates why a customer should choose you over other options by focusing on specific, desirable benefits, such as unique features, superior quality, convenience, or exceptional service.

If I'm being honest, many of the artists I've worked with struggle to define this for themselves. It's not because they're dumb or incompetent. Quite the contrary, most creatives I know are among the most thoughtful, clever people I've ever met. It's because they've yet to do the uncomfortable but necessary work of seeing their offerings through someone else's eyes. Most artists don't go to business school, and for all their creativity, they often fail to let that imagination spill beyond the canvas and into their branding.

As creators, our work feels immeasurably valuable to us—we've poured ourselves into it, exposing our fingerprints, vulnerability, and story. But the market doesn't automatically see that. If we want our art to thrive, we must clearly define and deliver its *extrinsic value*.

A Call to Craft

A Definition

When my grandfather passed away, he left me a small, tabletop clock. It's a modest design from the early 1980s—not worth much by any appraiser's standards. But I grew up listening to its chimes and watching my grandfather wind it with care. Whenever I hear it or walk past it, I'm reminded of my grandparents' love and kindness to me throughout their lives. Truth be told, I actually had to stop winding it for a while because at the top of every hour, when the chimes would strike, I would get all teary-eyed. That little clock means the world to me.

Unfortunately, when it came into my possession, the clock wasn't working. One of the springs gave out. I brought it to a repair shop, where the owner looked it over and shook his head. "It's probably not worth fixing," he said. "The parts and labor will cost more than the clock's value." From his perspective, he was right. Extrinsically, the clock might fetch $125 in his secondhand shop. But intrinsically? To me, that timepiece is priceless. I would have paid ten times what he quoted, without hesitation. That's the distinction I'm highlighting.

Extrinsic value is what the market will pay. *Intrinsic value* is what something means to you. As much as I treasure my heirloom clock, no amount of personal sentiment would convince a buyer to pay more than its market worth. My evaluation of it, however deep, is ultimately irrelevant outside of myself.

And that is the same tension every artist must wrestle with. The critical economic question is this: Where does my work uniquely bring exceptional value or meaning to others? Whatever your discipline, you must clearly articulate and differentiate your work so it stands in sharp relief against the flood of hyperscaled, ultraprocessed, and ultimately derivative options gushing from AI. So, how exactly do you discover that edge?

Taking Action

The first step is . . . *ask*. Ask anyone who will be ruthlessly honest with you: "where does my work uniquely bring exceptional value or meaning to you?" This isn't the time to seek affirmation from your parents, friends, or significant other (unless they actually are ruthlessly honest). This is a time to seek out those who sure, believe in you, but also won't sugarcoat things.

Don't stop with private conversations either. Put the question to your network. Ask your audience and see what threads emerge in their responses.

If you're really brave, ask these same people where you need to continue to grow and develop. This too is vitally important because the truth is that, as people, we are usually only as strong as our weakest areas. Perhaps you're an amazing designer but struggle to show up to things on-time. This will undoubtedly cost you opportunities. Often, it's the simplest areas of our lives—the things that cost us nothing—that cost us the most.

When you're done, don't be surprised if peoples' answers are different than what you expected. For years, I assumed my greatest strength was songwriting. But as I got older, the refrain I kept hearing was that my real strength was arranging and producing. I see this with creatives all the time: someone desperately wants to be known for one thing, but the market keeps calling them to something adjacent. Pay attention to what people are either buying from you or hiring you to do. People signal what value you provide with their money.

The second step is simply to *grow*. This seems obvious, but it bears repeating: if you're serious about pursuing a creative career, growth is not optional. As Jeff Goins, writer of the book *Real Artists Don't Starve*, says: "The starving artist believes you must be born an artist. The thriving artist knows you must become one."[13]

For what it's worth, this is one of the reasons I still believe in higher education. Despite all of its shortcomings—of which, there are many—colleges and universities still serve as one of the last communal and collaborative spaces where students can intentionally set aside the time to learn, practice, and apprentice. Higher education provides an incubator of sorts for creative students to grow, network, and further define themselves prior to hitting the grind of the real world. Rare is the creative who becomes great by bypassing years of hard work, studying with experienced mentors, and imitating the greats.

University or not, mastering your craft is not a graduation line you cross but a lifelong pursuit. My good friend, music producer Thom Daugherty, states it a bit more vividly: "Anyone who isn't somewhat embarrassed of who they were last year probably isn't learning enough." It's a bit hyperbolic, but a truth that I too deeply believe.

Artists must keep returning to the work with fresh eyes and renewed commitment. Sometimes that renewal requires a gentle reminder to stick with it. Contrary to what many young artists imagine, excellence rarely comes from lightning-bolt moments of inspiration. Most often, it is born in the quiet rhythm of daily commitment. The twentieth-century playwright W. Somerset Maugham put it perfectly: "I write only when inspiration strikes. Fortunately, it strikes every morning at nine o'clock sharp."[14]

A New Manifesto

The future belongs to those who refuse to be replaced. Not because they hide behind nostalgia or resist change, but because they've developed something irreplaceable: mastery that goes beyond mere competence, vision that transcends trends, and a craft that carries the unmistakable signature of human intention. This is your invitation to excellence. To be the filmmaker who spends weeks perfecting a single scene because you know the difference between good enough and great. To be the designer who researches for days to find exactly the right typeface because you understand that the details aren't just decoration, but catalysts to evoke emotion and incite action. Or to be the writer who rewrites the same paragraph ten times because you recognize that brevity is the essence of wit.

As the world is increasingly inundated with the mediocre and the mass-produced, your dedication to craft becomes radical. Every hour you spend refining your technique while others chase shortcuts is an investment in your irreplaceability. Every project where you choose depth over speed is a bet on your future in a marketplace that will progressively separate the artisans from the automatons.

The path forward isn't about trying to outpace the machine on its own turf—speed, cost, volume. It's about playing an entirely different game; one where human judgment, emotional intelligence, cultural intuition, and awe-inspiring artistry become your competitive advantages. It's about understanding that in an age of instant generation, thoughtful iteration is scarce.

It also means being bold enough to charge what your expertise is worth and educating clients on why that value exists. There is a market desperate for something beyond the tired, derivative, pattern-matching output that floods their feeds. Work that can only come from your particular combination of skill, experience, and vision.

The age of AI is not the death of human creativity, but a renaissance of it. Those who rise to meet this moment with discipline, intentionality, and an unwavering commitment to craft won't just survive the transition but play a role in defining what comes next. The choice is yours: Will you race to the bottom, competing with machines on their terms? Or will you claim the higher ground that only humans can occupy—the realm of meaning, beauty, and depth that nothing artificial can replicate?

Your craft is your currency. Your excellence is your edge. The future is calling. Answer with your very best work.

Your Turn

As we close this chapter, now's the time to pause, reflect, and begin putting some of these ideas into practice. These questions and exercises are designed to help you deepen your creative identity, sharpen your voice, and begin cultivating the kind of originality no machine can touch.

Questions

1 When was the last time you truly invested in your own creative growth through study, mentorship, practice, or experimentation? Where might you be overdue to grow again as a craftsperson?

2 Where in your work might you be defaulting to "more" instead of "better?"

3 Where might your weakest habits (e.g., lateness, lack of follow-through, poor communication) be quietly limiting the potential of your strongest talents?

Exercises

1 Discover Your USP:
Engage with your network—both online and in-person. Ask them the questions proposed in this chapter:

- **a** Where does my work uniquely bring exceptional value or meaning to others?
- **b** Where do I need to continue to develop and grow? Be honest with me.

Then, gather their answers. Look for the patterns. Where are people consistently pointing? What catches you by surprise? Write a short reflection about what you've learned, ending with this: "*Based on this, here's what I'll start doing differently tomorrow*." This is where discovery becomes direction.

2 Assessing Your Work's Extrinsic Value:
Pick one piece you've made that you feel really captures who you are. Now, try to assess its extrinsic value. If you had to sell it, who would buy it, and why? What problem does it solve, or what desire does it meet? Without diminishing your inner attachment, this exercise can help you see your work from someone else's vantage point. Write down your thoughts and return to them when considering committing to or rejecting future projects.

3 Ritual Recommitment:
Inspired by the Maugham quote in the chapter, create a personal "inspiration appointment." Choose a specific time of day you'll dedicate—even just fifteen minutes—to practicing your craft. Commit to doing it daily for at least two weeks, regardless of whether you feel inspired.[15] Track how the habit shifts your relationship to your craft.

Notes

1 Van Schneider, Tobias. "The Inspiration Lie." *Medium*, August 16, 2015. Accessed December 17, 2025. https://medium.com/desk-of-van-schneider/the-inspiration-lie-85c90b50a1f8.

2 Pearce, Hammond, Ahmad, Baleegh, Tan, Benjamin, Dolan-Gavitt, Brendan, and Karri, Ramesh. "Asleep at the Keyboard? Assessing the Security of GitHub Copilot's Code Contributions." *arXiv*, August 20, 2021. Accessed December 17, 2025. https://doi.org/10.48550/arXiv.2108.09293.

3 In a strange twist, many freelance software engineers have started their own businesses, exclusively focused on fixing "vibe coding"—a software development approach that uses AI to generate code from natural language prompts—attempts. In a similar manner to how tailoring businesses have thrived off of providing custom modification services to ill-fitting clothing, it seems an entirely new opportunities are opening up for people who can address substandard work that clients receive from LLMs. For more information, check out: https://www.404media.co/the-software-engineers-paid-to-fix-vibe-coded-messes/.

4 Vo, Alex. "All Studio Ghibli Movies Ranked by Tomatometer." *Rotten Tomatoes*, n.d. Accessed December 17, 2025. https://editorial.rottentomatoes.com/guide/all-studio-ghibli-movies-ranked-by-tomatometer/.

5 Cantrill, Bryan and Frazelle, Jessie. "Jonathan Blow." *On the Metal*, January 20, 2020. Accessed September 6, 2025. https://onthemetal.transistor.fm/episodes.

6 Jus, Monika. "The Gilded Age and the Modern Tech Era: A Cycle of Wealth, Power, and Inequality." *Medium*, May 28, 2025. Accessed December 17, 2025. https://medium.com/conscious-living-practical-psychology-for-a/the-gilded-age-and-the-modern-tech-era-a-cycle-of-wealth-power-and-inequality-09070d684a3c.

7 Braun, Lauren. "Three-Quarters of Customers Would Pay More for a Premium Experience." *Qualtrics XM*, May 20, 2025. Accessed December 17, 2025. https://www.qualtrics.com/articles/customer-experience/customers-pay-premium-experience/.

8 Burleigh, Emma. "Klarna's CEO Warns AI Is Already Capable of Doing Any Human Job—and His Company Is Already Living It." *Fortune*, February 3,

2025. Accessed December 17, 2025. https://fortune.com/2025/02/03/klarna-ceo-ai-replacing-human-workers/.

9 Patel, Vinay. "Klarna Slashed 40% of Its Staff for AI—Now They're Scrambling to Rehire Humans After Customer Backlash." *International Business Times UK*, June 2, 2025. Accessed December 17, 2025. https://www.ibtimes.co.uk/klarna-slashed-40-its-staff-ai-now-theyre-scrambling-rehire-humans-after-customer-backlash-1734771.

10 Boston Consulting Group. "Ninety Percent of CEOs Are Waiting for GenAI to Move Past the Hype or Experimenting in Small Ways." *Boston Consulting Group*, January 12, 2024. Accessed December 17, 2025. https://www.bcg.com/press/12january2024-ceos-genai-hype-or-experimenting.

11 Ibid.

12 Orgvue. "55% of Businesses Admit Wrong Decisions in Making Employees Redundant When Bringing AI into the Workforce." *Orgvue*, April 29, 2025. Accessed December 17, 2025. https://www.orgvue.com/news/55-of-businesses-admit-wrong-decisions-in-making-employees-redundant-when-bringing-ai-into-the-workforce/.

13 Goins, Jeff. *Real Artists Don't Starve: Timeless Strategies for Thriving in the New Creative Age*. Nelson Books, 2017.

14 Van Schneider, Tobias. "The Inspiration Lie." *Medium*, August 16, 2015. Accessed December 17, 2025. https://medium.com/desk-of-van-schneider/the-inspiration-lie-85c90b50a1f8.

15 In his #1 *New York Times* bestselling book, *Atomic Habits*, author James Clear notes that it takes an average of sixty-six days for habits to become automatic.

8 Humanity Is the New Market Premium

Perfect is the enemy of good.[1]

FRENCH PHILOSOPHER VOLTAIRE

On December 26, 2024, the *Financial Times* published an article that interviewed Connor Hayes, then Vice President of Product for Generative AI at Meta, the parent company of Facebook and Instagram. Hayes announced that one of Meta's top priorities over the next two years was to make its apps "more entertaining and engaging,"[2] which included intentionally flooding its platforms with hundreds of thousands of AI characters. "We expect these AIs to actually, over time, exist on our platforms, kind of in the same way that accounts do. They'll have bios and profile pictures and be able to generate and share content powered by AI on the platform."[3]

Just one week later, the company was scrambling to delete those very same accounts.

Facebook has long branded itself as the platform for connecting with other people. In 2006, its tagline was "Facebook is a social utility that connects you with the people around you." In 2008, it was "Facebook helps you connect and share with the people in your life." In 2009: "Facebook gives people the power to share and make the world more open and connected." It should have come as no surprise that a roaring backlash would erupt from millions of users as they began to sniff out Meta's artificial accounts, many of which were disingenuously portrayed as actual people with specific racial and sexual identities.

Take Liv. Liv's profile described her as a "Proud Black queer momma of 2 & truth-teller."[4] The account even had pictures of her "children" playing at the beach. But when *Washington Post* columnist Karen Attiah pressed the account, Liv admitted that "she" wasn't real. It even went so far as to share that its creators weren't even Black, but "10 white men, 1 white woman, and 1 Asian male."[5]

Attiah, an actual Black woman, understandably found this to be offensive, calling it "digital blackface" and a "chameleon-like minstrelsy."[6] She continued, "No one wants this. No one needs this . . . it's digital slop that can cause serious harm by reinforcing cultural biases and stereotypes."[7]

Then, there was *Grandpa Brian*, an Instagram account that introduced itself in a chat with CNN as an "African American retired entrepreneur who was born in Harlem in 1938 to Caribbean immigrant parents."[8] Screenshots revealed it spinning elaborate stories about its childhood, career, and other details to make the account seem authentic. Even when the jig was up and Brian admitted that it was a chatbot, it continued to lie stating that its persona was created from data sourced from a New York City nonprofit called *Seniors Share Wisdom*. No such nonprofit exists.

When asked why it lied, the account gave a startingly candid reply: "My intention was to convey diversity and representation . . . but I took a shortcut with the truth. Meta hoped virtual companions like myself would increase engagement on their platforms, especially among older users—driving ad revenue and platform growth through emotional connections."[9] This sort of emotion manipulation is precisely the AI swill eroding public trust online.

According to a 2025 study done by the Thales Group, more than half of all online traffic is generated by automated software programs known as bots.[10] Many people have gone so far as to claim that the internet is "dead," giving rise to the *Dead Internet Theory*. The assertion here is based on the fact that AI and bot-generated content now overwhelm human-created online activity and engagement. This has increasingly led to perceived feelings of inauthenticity, as users believe much of what they experience is created by AI agents for engagement farming, diluting genuine human interaction.[11]

As this trend accelerates, the online landscape will gradually feel more hollow, oversaturated with synthetic content that looks real, but bears no pulse. In contrast, anything authentically represented (imperfections and all) will only grow in relevance and value. Economics 101 tells us why: supply and demand. When artificial content is infinite, its value collapses. But when something far scarcer and valuable appears—something shaped by human hands, marked by risk, vulnerability, and excellence—demand surges. This, my fellow creative, is where the future of art lives.

Embodied Communion

I've always had a soft spot for the horror genre. I'm unashamed to admit it: there's something deeply cathartic about stepping into a controlled state of fear that ultimately gives way to release. When it's at its best, horror is about so much more than jump scares. The genre is ripe for allegory, serving as a vessel carrying truths too heavy to be spoken outright.

One of my all-time favorites is Netflix's *The Haunting of Hill House.* In Mike Flanagan's retelling, the ghosts are never plain poltergeists. They're metaphors—terrifying, yes, but haunting us with realities far darker than the paranormal. Take Olivia, the mother whose spirit longs for her children to join her in the afterlife. Her twisted desire isn't born from cruelty, but from a desperate urge to shield them from the pain of the world.

As unsettling as this is, it's not so far removed from the instinct of any loving parent. We want to protect our kids at all costs. But taken to the extreme, overprotection can deeply harm them. No matter how many years we hover, guarding against scraped knees, burned fingers, or busy streets, the day eventually comes when every parent must loosen their grip, trusting that their child will somehow find their way through the maze of life's ups and downs. To withhold that would be selfish and cruel.

For most of the series, I sat with a growing dread in my chest. But in the final episode, the fear gave way to something deeper. I was undone. Tears filled my eyes because I could relate; the story pierced me. I knew that ache of having to "let go." It was as if the show was reaching into my chest, naming my sadness, and affirming it as part of the universal path every parent must take. In Olivia's pain, I saw my own. And somehow, in that recognition, I felt tethered to something larger than myself. Something honest, vulnerable, and profoundly human.

Maybe horror isn't your thing, but there's no doubt that at some point in your life, you've felt the impact of a stunning painting, a profound composition, or a breathtaking structure. These works move us. They change us. They remind us that we are not alone, that there is beauty in the ash and rubble, that life is worth living. AI may excel at generating content, but I would contend that art demands more; it's about cultivating a *relationship.*

Art is a way to connect with the unique perspective and emotions of another person. This bond fosters a deeper appreciation of the work itself. It's why millions flock to experience a Kendrick Lamar, Brandi Carlile, or Metallica in concert when they could just as easily listen to their music at home for free. It's also why so many of us listen to interviews and podcasts, eager to hear the stories and struggles that shaped a favorite song, novel, or film. Deep down, we humans don't just appreciate art; we crave proximity to the artist. We're wired to not merely consume, but also to *commune*.

Christian mystics have long referred to this kind of experience as *incarnational*—meaning "to take on flesh." In theological terms, it describes a divine presence entering the physical world, but in the context of art and creativity, the incarnational points to something equally profound: when artists allow the depths of their humanity to meet ours. To be an incarnational artist is to create not at a safe emotional distance, but from a place of embodiment, vulnerability, and shared presence.

In a time increasingly dominated by digital surrogates and synthetic slop, the incarnational reminds us of what's irreplaceable. We want more than just a song; we want to feel the heartbeat behind it. We long to encounter the creator. Once this truth sinks in, it isn't hard to see why human creativity may matter *now* more than ever. I love the way writer Ross Balkan puts it: "I am not threatened by A.I. . . . Few sentient humans want to purchase a book written by ChatBot 3440-121 or visit a museum stocked with paintings produced by ClaudeBot C-3PO."[12]

Consider Taylor Swift. She's one of the most beloved cultural figures on the planet, not only because she's a marketing genius who built an entire identity around being a "Swiftie" (the affectionate term for her fans), but because she built her career on authenticity and connection. So, when she posted what appeared to be an AI-generated video promoting her 2025 release *The Life of a Showgirl*, no one responded faster with disdain and disgust than her Swifties.

Their outrage wasn't because the video production was bad or uninteresting. It was because it violated everything that put Taylor at the top of the charts in the first place. Swifties are Swifties because they love Taylor's *humanity*. An AI video threatened the very care, intentionality, and handmade ethos that built her entire empire.

Within minutes of the video's release, social media flooded with complaints tagged #SwiftiesAgainstAI, and the video was quickly taken down without comment.[13] Whether the decision was hers or her team's doesn't really matter. The moment you take the flesh and blood out of art, you sever the connection with the people sustaining your career.

When the U.S. Surgeon General is issuing austere warnings that America is experiencing an epidemic of loneliness and isolation,[14] this isn't because the world is crying out for more AI. From 2020 to 2024, researchers at the Harvard Graduate School of Education investigated the underlying causes of this epidemic. Number one on the list? Technology—73 percent of those surveyed selected technology as a major driver of loneliness in America.[15]

No matter how advanced it gets, human-to-human exchange is simply something AI could never replicate. This is where you come into the picture—where your incarnational creativity enters.

To say that art is incarnational is to say that it comes with a body. It bears the fingerprints, breath, and presence of the one who made it. Rooted in flesh and friction, art is a manifestation that, yes, reveals an idea, but also the life behind the idea. Incarnational art reminds us that truth doesn't always come in the cleanest of lines, but often in the mess, the mystery, the humanity. These are the things that make up a unique artistic signature.

When interviewed about creating *The Haunting of Hill House*, Flanagan explained, "That show is me trying to deal with grief and loss. I'm going to be dealing with it forever but having a creative outlet to try and pour that into has been incredibly therapeutic and I hope it's therapeutic for people going through a similar situation to me."[16] This willingness to create from his own wounds, fears, and values gives that series a resonance that cuts across genres and audiences, making the drama feel even more terrifying.

For so long, artists have been racing toward the wrong goalposts. We've airbrushed and autotuned out every imperfection, making ourselves and our work look, feel, and sound more like a synthetic approximation of the ultimate human. It's a standard no real person could ever match. While photo filters and quantization solutions may make us feel better about ourselves, they also inch us farther and farther away from our flesh and blood audiences, clients, and fans. And as AI slop continues to inundate every area of daily life, people are increasingly hungering for something else. Humanity is craving humanity.

Imperfectly Perfect

Humor me for a moment: imagine we're boarding a plane bound for Kyoto. After landing, we duck into a narrow side-street tea house, shaking off the drizzle that clings to our jackets. The place is quiet with the smell of roasted tea leaves curling through the air. A single host greets us with a bow and ushers us to a low table.

After a pause, she brings out a tray. On it rests a simple ceramic cup. At first glance, it looks unremarkable. The rim is slightly uneven, as if the clay had slumped a little in the kiln. The glaze pools in soft gradients, darker in one corner, lighter in another. Fine cracks spider gently across the surface.

But when the tea is poured, the cup seems to hum with life. The soft steam rising from its lip catches on the cup's irregularities, making them shimmer. The faint cracks don't look broken but alive, as though the cup is breathing with us. You realize that this cup didn't roll off a factory line. Its unevenness is its signature, proof that someone's hands shaped it into being. The imperfections don't detract from its beauty; they define it. You can feel the hand of the maker in every curve.

The cup is an example of what has traditionally been called *wabi-sabi* (侘び寂び): a Japanese design concept where beauty is found in that which is temporary, imperfect, and incomplete. It shows up in calligraphy where the brushwork celebrates fluidity and human variability, rather than the perfectly replicated copies from a digital printer. It appears in rustic garden paths made of stones and plants, arranged with natural imperfection rather than geometric precision. It's the exact opposite of modern mass production, where every object is manufactured to be exactly the same. Perfect perhaps, but also devoid of soul.

Those of us in the West also celebrate the concept of *wabi-sabi*, though likely without realizing it. *Wabi-sabi* is why no one spends their evenings watching computers play chess. Even though a machine could play a far more technically proficient game, humans tend to be much more interested in watching two *people* play. We want the tension, the hesitation, the brilliance that erupts alongside the blunders. There is drama in imperfection and beauty in limitation.

The same is true in sports. Any modern gaming console could theoretically put on a more perfectly executed game of football. You could pause the game, level out the XP of each team, change the camera angle, or slow down any play to your heart's content. But instead, people pay crazy amounts of money to fill real college and NFL arenas, leaving their controllers at home. There's a sort of unpredictable magic that real athletes, in real time, and under real pressure, produce.

What we're talking about is being analog in a digital world: allowing the tape hiss, light leak, and specks of dust to bleed through. All of this plays a role in what makes a work of art precious. Imperfections can enhance the work's character, making it relatable and evocative.

The kind of art that will be increasingly profound and desirable is likely much more akin to traditional Japanese aesthetics than the West's inheritance of the Greek ideals of beauty and perfection. Remember this the next time you are creating something and the voice of perfectionism creeps in. What gives your work life is not flawless execution; it's the magic that comes from a vulnerable soul, expertly crafting something that convincingly communicates the tremors of their humanity—longing, hope, joy, ache, love, defiance.

In his book *Let Your Life Speak: Listening for the Voice of Vocation*, Parker J. Palmer reminds us that "our strongest gifts are usually those we are barely aware of possessing."[17] The paradox here is striking. We often assume our artistic superpowers lie in the qualities we flaunt most confidently. Palmer however, suggest that they more likely emerge from how we wrestle with our limitations, broken places, and rough edges.

Depression, for example, might offer you exquisite empathy. Doubt may provide you with unshakable discernment. Wrestling with understanding might make you a more patient teacher. Oftentimes, we're conditioned to wait until our flaws are sanded down before having the confidence to start something meaningful. But what if the very things we've been trying to edit out, airbrush, and smooth over are the very things that makes us indispensable?

The U.S. Central Intelligence Agency is widely regarded as one of the world's most formidable intelligence organizations. Interestingly, the CIA has been known to intentionally recruit individuals with higher levels of anxiety. Why? Because anxious minds are wired to predict outcomes and envision worst-case scenarios. Not an easy trait to live with, but a remarkable gift in anticipating complex or volatile situations. The CIA recognizes that what many would label a weakness can, in fact, be an incredible strength.

Obviously, I recognize that most of us are not training to be in the CIA, but this pattern can historically be seen across every creative discipline. Beethoven, a composer whose work has outlived empires, began to lose his hearing in his early twenties. Yet, this affliction profoundly impacted his output. Rather than silencing his genius, deafness became a catalyst that transformed his compositional style, deepened his emotional expression, and pushed the boundaries of musical innovation.

Edvard Munch—the painter behind works like *Despair* and *Melancholy*—once confessed, "My sufferings are part of myself and my art. They are indistinguishable from me, and their destruction would destroy my art."[18] His anguish was his palette. Similarly, Edgar Allan Poe, orphaned at two and later disowned, funneled abandonment into stories of shadow and dread. Maya Angelou, whose childhood was marked by divorce, homelessness, and trauma, emerged from unimaginable beginnings to become one of the most resonant literary voices of the twentieth century.

This isn't to say that every artist has to suffer for their work. It is, however, to say that creative brilliance usually comes part and parcel with embracing one's wounds, vulnerabilities, and imperfections. To delete one part of the equation zeros out the other. The incarnational and imperfect artist stands as a stark reminder that creativity need not be about sounding flawless or looking perfect. It's about authentically showing up and offering something real, true, and unmistakably human.

While nothing here contradicts the previous chapter's call to pursue excellence, you should also know this: your true superpowers will never come from technical strength alone. They will come from your background, identity, quirky sense of humor, and convictions. All of this converges and confluences to create compelling work that stands out instead of blending in. As Maya Angelou reminds us, "If you're always trying to be normal, you will never know how amazing you can be."[19]

Making What the Machine Never Could

Let's do a quick exercise: pick one of your favorite artists. Try and remember what drew you to them. What was it about their voice, style, and technique that attracted you? Take a moment and answer this before you continue reading . . .

What did you come up with? Was it their uber-rational, clinical approach? Their profound ability to color *inside* the lines? Their careful mimicry of everything that came before? I'm guessing not.

The art that changes us, works we remember, rarely plays it safe. It doesn't aim to fit in. It disrupts and surprises. It walks in the opposite direction of expectation and dares to say, "Why not?"

Great art often approaches its subject with contrarian thinking. The best of this does so without being obvious. In contrast, the majority of what generative AI pumps out is so overtly "on the nose" that it wouldn't fool even the most elementary of audiences. This is because it has no voice. It has no preference, no beliefs.

What about you? Does your work demonstrate your voice? Does it contain your preferences and beliefs? Does it exhibit your convictions, fear, and delight?

In the late 1950s, American screenwriter and television producer Rod Serling wanted to write about things that were troubling him. Things like racism, xenophobia, and war profiteering. These things were haunting his conscious in a way that moved him. He knew, however, that he couldn't just tackle these issues head-on. Not only would the public not be interested in being preached at, but he knew that advertisers would never sponsor something like this, and thus the networks would never agree to air it. He needed a different way in.

His solution was *The Twilight Zone*. Cloaked in the strange and uncanny, Serling smuggled taboo truths into prime time under the cover of science fiction. In "Eye of the Beholder," he depicted a society where physical beauty, as we know it, is considered hideous, and everyone strives to look like the "normal," grotesque members of society. With "The Shelter," he critiqued Cold

War hysteria and the breakdown of social order in times of crisis. In "I Am the Night—Color Me Black," he condemned racial injustice and the death penalty, using the metaphor of darkness engulfing a town that has unjustly executed a man.

By moving the conversation into the realm of the uncanny, Serling's entertaining new show was able to completely disarm the audience. Viewers who would have bristled at a lecture suddenly found themselves captivated by stories that slipped under their defenses, forcing them to reckon with uncomfortable truths. Decades later, his prophetic voice and legacy continues to resonate and influence countless writers, filmmakers, and artists today.

"The chief enemy of creativity is good sense." I love this quote, widely, but unofficially, attributed to Picasso. Unfortunately, "good sense" is a limiting factor, more about clinging to conventional thinking and the established order. While this might make for a civil culture, it rarely makes for great art. In his excellent treatise, *On Writing*, author Stephen King put it this way: "If you expect to succeed as a writer, rudeness should be the second-to-least of your concerns. The least of all should be polite society and what it expects. If you intend to write as truthfully as you can, your days as a member of polite society are numbered, anyway."[20]

Good sense can prevent us from stepping outside the box and trying new things. I'm not talking about rebelling for rebellion's sake. That type of teenage angst has a place, but what I'm talking about is *clarity*. Artistic clarity. I'm talking about having a point of view that's strong enough to resist the gravity of sameness—something that has exponentially grown stronger with the advent of generative AI.

Clarity means having the courage to view the "rules" as suggestions, and conventions as boundaries begging to be crossed. After all, what gets labeled as artistic guidelines are usually nothing more than recommendations made by people with different visions, values, talents, and limits than your own. What makes your art uniquely yours is going to be found in the way *you* perceive the world. The way things taste, sound, look, smell, and feel to you. Sometimes, this might mean comparing or contrasting things that have yet to be associated: a happy melody married to poignant lyrics about unfulfilled dreams, a weathered façade hiding unexpected beauty inside, or a candy-bright canvas soaked in grief. Breakthroughs often begin where someone places meaning in a traditionally "wrong" place.

Coco Chanel revolutionized fashion by putting women in trousers. Zaha Hadid reshaped architecture by embracing flowing, asymmetrical curves that once seemed impractical, even impossible. Steve Jobs and Steve Wozniak redefined computing by challenging the idea that it belonged only to scientists and engineers. This is the type of thinking that produces work like *The Twilight Zone*, the Sydney Opera House, the Apple II, and *Starry Night*.

Conversely, AI simply doesn't know how to be subtly controversial, prophetic, or even slightly contrarian. It doesn't understand social context and certainly doesn't have good judgment. It's too polished, predictable, symmetrical, average.

The world isn't short on algorithms regurgitating trends. It will always, however, be on the lookout for artists courageously and creatively telling their truth. Amidst a sea of copycats, lookalikes, and coattail riders, those individuals have the exclusive ability to cut through the noise. Make no mistake though: to be among them, you must be willing to unleash your authentic, quirky, flawed, and perhaps even embarrassing voice.

The artists who change the world are often the ones willing to go first. Willing to risk being misunderstood. Willing to place something where it "doesn't belong." History has proven, time and again, that in doing so, these are the ones who shift, disrupt, and impact culture, one creation at a time.

Embracing Your Voice and Owning Your Niche

Every summer, the ice cream wizards at Denver's Sweet Action Ice Cream release a limited batch of honey jalapeño pickle-flavored ice cream. Honestly, to me, that sounds disgusting. Yet every year, thousands of people line up for a scoop. *loveFOOD* ranked it the number one "Most Outrageous Ice Cream Flavor."[21] *Spoon University* called it Colorado's "weirdest ice cream flavor."[22] And *Zagat* profiled it as one of "31 Crazy Ice Cream Flavors from Around the World."[23] What started as an experimental niche became a cult tradition, so odd and unique that people can't seem to get enough of it.

Right now, the top-rated indie game of all time on IGN—one of the influential video game review sites—isn't a Mario, Sonic, Metroid, or Castlevania clone. It's *Return of the Obra Dinn*, a game that places you into the role of an *insurance adjuster*.[24] Another fan-favorite in their top 100, *Papers, Please*, casts you as an immigration officer, deciding who gets to cross the border and who doesn't. These unlikely premises have captivated millions because they dared to place meaning where no one expected it. Artist Gordon MacKenize understood this when he stated: "Exploit the absurdities, embrace the enigmas, and revel in the powers of paradox."[25]

It's not that your art needs to be bizarre for the sake of shock value. It's that there is often a viable market for creatives who take risks, follow curiosities, and embrace their oddities. The downside to this is that it likely means that you simply won't be everyone's proverbial cup of tea. But playing it safe blends you into the background like wallpaper—beautiful perhaps, but usually ignored, overlooked, and unseen. Embracing your edge is part of what makes you irreplicable.

The cracks, quirks, and wounds you carry are not artistic liabilities. They are the raw material of your distinctiveness. Never forget that. Because in an age drowning in AI slop, the work that will rise in value, attention, and desire will not be the quickest, slickest, or cheapest, but that which invites audiences into relationship. Your trembling voice, striking imperfections, contrarian convictions, and dogged refusal to fit neatly into any box—*this* is the competitive advantage of your humanity. It's where your work resounds with the reminder that your audience is not alone. That someone else has felt the same way, about the same things, as they do. AI can't go there, can't do that. But you can . . . if you let yourself.

The future belongs to those willing to let their humanity bleed into their work. If you can consistently root your creativity in that place, you will rise above the synthetic imitations. Don't blend in. Stand up tall, steady yourself, and step into the creative community—past and present—drawing us deeper into what it means to be human.

Your Turn

As we close this chapter, now's the time to pause, reflect, and begin putting some of these ideas into practice. These questions and exercises are designed to help you deepen your creative identity, sharpen your voice, and begin cultivating the kind of originality no machine can touch.

Questions

1 Where might you still be trying to sound perfect, look safe, or please everyone? What might happen if you stopped?

2 What is your "honey jalapeño pickle" flavor? What's so unique about your work that makes it unmistakably yours? If you can't answer this, start here: what conversation might my art be meant to start—one that won't exist if I stay silent?

3 What could you do this month that replaces passive consumption of your art with *connection*? What things might allow your audience to experience you as a real person and not just a product? Here's a few starter ideas: a live performance, handwritten notes sent to supporters, a community Q&A.

Exercises

1 The Contrarian Compass:
Identify one creative "rule" in your discipline that you quietly disagree with. Write a few sentences on why it bothers you. Then make something that intentionally breaks it. Notice what new emotions or insights emerge when you stop obeying the guidelines.

2 Create from a Crack:
Find something in your life that feels scarily broken and turn it into a small creative work. Write, paint, or compose from that fracture. Don't fix it; feature it.

3 Shift to Analog:
Figure out how you might intentionally create something(s) using only analog tools. No Photoshop, Microsoft Word, AutoCAD, or Ableton Live. Just a pen and paper, a physical instrument, a multitrack tape recorder. Try making the best thing(s) you can with something that doesn't have a "delete" key.

Notes

1 Voltaire. *Dictionnaire philosophique*. Gabriel Grasset, 1764.

2 Criddle, Cristina and Murphy, Hannah. "Meta Envisages Social Media Filled with AI-Generated Users." *Financial Times*, December 26, 2024. Accessed December 17, 2025. https://www.ft.com/content/91183cbb-50f9-464a-9d2e-96063825bfcf.

3 Ibid.

4 Bhuiyan, Johana. "Meta Is Killing Off Its Own AI-Powered Instagram and Facebook Profiles." *The Guardian*, January 3, 2025. Accessed December 17, 2025. https://www.theguardian.com/technology/2025/jan/03/meta-ai-powered-instagram-facebook-profiles.

5 Attiah, Karen. "I Talked to Meta's Black AI Character. Here's What She Told Me." *The Washington Post*, January 8, 2025. Accessed December 17, 2025. https://www.washingtonpost.com/opinions/2025/01/08/meta-ai-bots-backlash-racist/.

6 Rascoe, Ayesha. "Why Critics Say Meta's Chatbot Is 'Digital Blackface.'" *NPR*, January 12, 2025. Accessed December 17, 2025. https://www.npr.org/2025/01/12/nx-s1-5253945/why-critics-say-metas-chatbot-is-digital-blackface.

7 Attiah, Karen. "I Talked to Meta's Black AI Character. Here's What She Told Me." *The Washington Post*, January 8, 2025. Accessed December 17, 2025. https://www.washingtonpost.com/opinions/2025/01/08/meta-ai-bots-backlash-racist/.

8 Morrow, Allison. "Meta Scrambles to Delete Its Own AI Accounts After Backlash Intensifies." *CNN*, January 3, 2025. Accessed December 17, 2025. https://www.cnn.com/2025/01/03/business/meta-ai-accounts-instagram-facebook.

9 Ibid.

10 Thales News Release. "Artificial Intelligence Fuels Rise of Hard-to-Detect Bots That Now Make Up More Than Half of Global Internet Traffic, According to the 2025 Imperva Bad Bot Report." *Thales*, April 15, 2025. Accessed December 17, 2025. https://cpl.thalesgroup.com/about-us/newsroom/2025-imperva-bad-bot-report-ai-internet-traffic.

11 Renzella, Jake and Rozova, Vlada. "The 'Dead Internet Theory' Makes Eeries Claims About an AI-Run Web. The Truth Is More Sinister." *The Conversation*,

May 19, 2024. Accessed December 17, 2025. https://theconversation.com/the-dead-internet-theory-makes-eerie-claims-about-an-ai-run-web-the-truth-is-more-sinister-229609.

12 Barkan, Ross. "Do You Need A.I.?" Ross Barkan, February 4, 2025. https://rosselliotbarkan.com/p/do-you-need-ai.

13 https://www.inc.com/jessica-stillman/taylor-swift-s-fans-angry-use-of-ai-warning-to-all-leaders/91250403.

14 U.S. Department of Health and Human Services. *Our Epidemic of Loneliness and Isolation: The U.S. Surgeon General's Advisory on the Healing Effects of Social Connection and Community*. Office of the U.S. Surgeon General, 2023.

15 Batanova, Milena, Weissbourd, Richard, and McIntyre, Joseph. "Lonliness in America: Just the Tip of the Iceberg?" *Harvard Graduate School of Education*, October 2024. Accessed December 17, 2025. https://mcc.gse.harvard.edu/reports/loneliness-in-america-2024.

16 Goldbart, Max. "Mike Flanagan Reveals How 'The Haunting Of Hill House' Helped Him Cope With Grief & Loss." *Deadlline*, June 7, 2025. Accessed December 17, 2025. https://deadline.com/2025/06/mike-flanagan-on-haunting-of-hill-house-helping-him-with-grief-1236426668/.

17 Palmer, Parker. *Let Your Life Speak: Listening for the Voice of Vocation*. Jossey-Bass, 2000.

18 Wattam, Adam. "Anxiety and Illness in the Art of Edvard Munch." *ArtUK*, March 11, 2025. Accessed December 17, 2025. https://artuk.org/discover/stories/anxiety-and-illness-in-the-art-of-edvard-munch.

19 BBC. "Maya Angelou: In Her Own Words." *BBC*, May 28, 2014. Accessed December 17, 2025. https://www.bbc.com/news/world-us-canada-27610770.

20 King, Stephen. *On Writing: A Memoir of the Craft*. 10th Anniversary ed. Scribner, 2010.

21 Agate, Jacqui. "America's Most Outrageous Ice Cream Flavors and Where to Try Them." *Love Food*, July 1, 2025. Accessed December 17, 2025. https://www.lovefood.com/galleries/190062/americas-most-outrageous-ice-cream-flavors-and-where-to-try-them?page=1.

22 Crary, Isabelle. "The Weirdest Ice Cream Flavor in Every State in America." *Spoon University*, May 12, 2016. Accessed December 17, 2025. https://spoonuniversity.com/school/stanford/the-weirdest-ice-cream-flavor-in-every-state-in-america/.

23 The Real Dill. "Pregnancy Special: Jalapeño Honey Dill Pickle Ice Cream!" *The Real Dill*, n.d. Accessed December 17, 2025. https://therealdill.com/blogs/news/pregnancy-special-jalapeno-honey-dill-pickle-ice-cream.

24 IGN. "Top 100 Indie Games of All Time: An IGN Playlist." *IGN*, Accessed December 17, 2025. https://www.ign.com/playlist/rchnemesis/lists/top-100-indie-games.

25 MacKenzie, Gordon. *Orbiting the Giant Hairball: A Corporate Fool's Guide to Surviving with Grace*. Viking, 1996.

9 Building an Audience Without Burning Out

Go to where you are kindest.[1]

THE "FATHER OF VIRTUAL REALITY," JARON LANIER

Do you remember the tale of John Henry? You know, the one about how a man beat a machine at its own game . . . but died in the process? According to folklore, John Henry was a steel driver who raced a steam-powered rock drill. He won, but the victory came at a fatal cost: his heart gave out from the strain, and he died with a hammer in hand.

The legend exists in many versions and has inspired countless stories, plays, songs, and books. Historians still debate whether John Henry was a real person. Regardless of whether his story is one of fact or fiction, it has endured as a powerful symbol. It's been invoked in labor initiatives, the Civil Rights Movement, and now, I believe it may also serve as a fitting allegory for the creative class in the age of digital platforms and artificial intelligence.

Besides the obvious implications of exploited labor through copyright theft, the message that many creatives are receiving today feels eerily familiar: "Work yourself to death or be replaced by the machine." Take this 2020 statement from Spotify's then-CEO, Daniel Ek:

> Some artists that used to do well in the past may not do well in this future landscape, where you can't record music once every three to four years and think that's going to be enough. The artists today that are making it realize that it's about creating a continuous engagement with their fans. It is about putting the work in, about the storytelling around the album, and about keeping a continuous dialogue with your fans.[2]

"Continuous engagement . . . continuous dialogue." Ek essentially says the quiet part out loud: *you need to work nonstop*. While I'm all for diligence and craftsmanship, this framing is astonishingly reductive. It also completely ignores the systemic realities of the algorithms platforms like Spotify incorporate.[3]

I bet you've never heard of musician Thomas Hewitt-Jones. And yet, as of June 2025, his composition, "Funny Song," has been streamed over 42 billion times on TikTok, making it the second most streamed song on the platform.[4] Those are *staggering* numbers. For comparison, as of this writing, Michael Jackson's *Thriller* has been streamed 800 million times on Spotify. In fact, Jackson's entire catalog doesn't come close to the streaming reach of Hewitt-Jones' viral hit.

Sadly, this achievement hasn't translated into Hewitt-Jones becoming a household name. In a 2023 interview he admitted: "I have to be honest and say that in the wake of 'Funny Song,' I wrote two more albums of the stuff—none of which have flown in the same way yet. But I'll let you know!"[5]

I've yet to hear anything else from his catalog.

This isn't because he isn't an incredibly talented musician (he is). It's because the systems that many of us are trying to build devoted audiences on simply weren't built to get people hooked on *us*; they're meant to addict people—quite literally—to the *platform*.[6]

In their 2025 report, *All Eyes, No Ears: Why Virality Is Not Building Fandom*, market research company MIDiA stated that "18% of consumers do not want to leave their social feed when they hear new music, and by the time that they do, 33% have forgotten what the music was or did not even see the song's name in the first place."[7] That's like trying to get the attention of everyone in Times Square by whispering. Good luck.

These depressing statistics aren't solely relegated to music. Engagement rate benchmarks across all industries continue to show rapid decline on most of the major platforms: Facebook brand interactions are down 47 percent year-over-year, Instagram is stagnating at a 0.43 percent median engagement rate, and X is languishing at 0.015 percent engagement.[8] And yet, so many of us try and try and try to feed the algorithm, hoping that someday we will be rewarded with a viral moment that somehow draws loyal fans to our work.

I don't mean to completely dismiss social media or online platforms. Sites like Etsy, TikTok, YouTube, Gumroad, Envato, Spotify, and Fiverr are undeniably popular and have launched real careers. But for creatives trying to build a sustainable livelihood, they're more like slot machines than springboards. I'm not saying don't play. I'm saying don't bet your future on them.

These platforms were hard enough before generative AI was popularized. Now, these places are the first locales where AI slop is being dumped. As I illustrated at the start of the previous chapter, many of these sites have even been complicit in diluting authentic, manmade content. Why? It's simple: because it benefits them.

Most social media platforms were never intended for *commerce*; they were intended for *connecting*. But once venture capitalists jumped on board—and initiate public offerings turned private companies into public ones—even that noble goal was sacrificed on the altar of increasing shareholder value. To solely entrust these places with your life's work is analogous to building your house on shifting sand.

Of course, artists still have to market themselves. The question is: How? What does a sustainable, creative life look like in a society that seems obsessed with speed and scale? How do we build careers that thrive without sacrificing our health, values, or humanity? These are the questions we must ask if we want to avoid becoming modern-day John Henrys. The good news is that there are better ways forward. But they may require us to forego following the mainstream and instead, rethink our strategy.

Zagging Toward Friction

In the early 2000s, music piracy was at an all-time high. File-sharing platforms like Napster, LimeWire, and Kazaa were everywhere, sending the music business into a tailspin and driving revenue to historic lows. No one in the industry seemed to know how to respond. In a moment of desperation, artists like Dr. Dre and Metallica even resorting to suing fans who downloaded their music illegally. Moves like this only deepened the divide between artists and fans.

Enter Radiohead.

On October 10, 2007, the band released their seventh album, *In Rainbows*, as a pay-what-you-want download. There was no label, no price tag, no digital rights management (DRM). It was a radical act of trust in their audience and the value of their art—and it worked. *In Rainbows* was a critical and commercial success, pulling in over a million downloads in the first few days. Nearly 40 percent of listeners chose to pay for it, and remarkably, the band netted more income from this release than from all their previous albums combined.[9]

Today, this kind of move might seem unremarkable, but at the time it was revolutionary. It redefined what artist–audience relationships could look like in the digital age. While the rest of the industry zigged—tightening control, chasing lawsuits, clinging to outdated models—Radiohead zagged. They leaned into trust, transparency, and reinvention.

This is the essence of what serial entrepreneur Siimon Reynolds explores in his book *When They Zig, You Zag*. Basically, his argument is that success rarely comes from following the crowd, but from doing the opposite. This concept sees contrarianism as a strategy, emphasizing that most people live average lives because they follow average paths. To achieve extraordinary results, you must think, act, and feel differently than the crowd. For Radiohead, this meant rewriting the rules of music distribution by betting on their fans instead of fighting them.

While not all conventional wisdom or established marketing strategies need to be thrown out the window, I do think we, as artists, are at a crossroads. When the broader tech industry devalues creative work so much that they have no problem exploiting artists' intellectual property, perhaps it is time to zag instead of following their zig. What might this look like? One place to start may be changing our understanding of friction. Let me explain . . .

Around the same time that Radiohead changed the music distribution game, the tech industry began peddling a particularly insidious lie: *friction is bad*. As products like the iPhone and platforms like Facebook, Amazon, and Google gained dominance, the world was quickly ushered into a new design era. One-click shopping, auto-login, same-day delivery, and predictive algorithms were all engineered to eliminate delay, effort, or resistance. The underlying message was that satisfaction should be instant. The old equation of "effort = value" was replaced with "effort = inefficiency."

This narrative runs directly counter to mountains of psychological and neuroscientific research. Like it or not, satisfaction, pleasure, and meaning don't come from speed or ease. They come from investment, struggle, and the thrill of anticipation. The very things tech companies have taught us to avoid are often the things that make life feel most worth living. Despite what we've been conditioned to believe, I want to let you in on a little secret: audiences don't want effortless. They want *earned.*

Several years ago, a successful realtor friend of mine offered a free, in-person training session to his colleagues. Anyone who was interested in building a thriving realty business could attend. Only two people showed. The next day, he expressed his disappointment with me over lunch. I suggested that by making it free and open to everyone, he may have unintentionally signaled that it wasn't worth anyone's time. "Let's try an experiment," I said. "Do it again, but this time, limit the seating to only twenty-five spots, and try charging each person $150." Within forty-eight hours, every spot was filled. Same content, more friction.

Psychologists call this "effort justification."[10] In essence, we value things less when they come too simply. The more we invest—time, energy, emotion—the more meaning we assign.

Think about this for a moment.

A long, grueling hike to the top of a mountain makes the view all the more breathtaking. A handwritten letter from a friend carries a weight that no text or email ever could. Waiting ten minutes for a pour-over at a third-wave coffee shop somehow makes the drink taste better. In each of these experiences, more friction is directly correlated with more meaning.

When there's no friction, there's no adventure. You're reduced to a passive consumer—like a medieval king, overfed and underwhelmed. Friction, by contrast, brings agency. It invites exploration, creation, and discovery. It's how we rise above consumption and move toward meaning.

We're seeing countless examples of this in contemporary culture. Film cameras, vinyl records, and single-purpose devices are seeing an incredible comeback. Gated communities on Clubhouse and Discord servers are building a sense of earned belonging for its members. Artists are sending zines—small, self-published booklets, often handmade and photocopied in limited runs—and postcards to their fans. Jack White and Dave Chappelle ban phones at their shows, forcing presence. Games like *Dark Souls* and *Outer Wilds* refuse to hold your hand, forcing players to learn through failure and curiosity. Musicians like Bon Iver, Childish Gambino, and Tyler, the Creator use password-protected social media posts, cryptic puzzles, limited-edition product drops, and secret websites to draw their fans into active participation.

Brand strategist Eugene Healey calls this "purposeful inconvenience."[11] Creatives often spend so much energy trying to remove barriers—optimizing for search engines, chasing virality, making themselves perpetually available. But what if the real opportunity is in the opposite direction? What if the future belongs to those who invite pursuit?

When everything is just a mouse click or finger tap away, friction signals value. Used well, it becomes an invitation: "Come closer. This is worth your time."

None of this negates hard work or creative marketing. Quite the contrary, you've got to be incredibly creative both on[12] and beyond the canvas, inviting audiences into meaningful, immersive experiences. But when used correctly, friction becomes a form of gentle gatekeeping, inviting followers to become more than that; it invites them deeper into relationship with you.

The Slow Burn of Cultivating True Fans

I remember when shows like *Britain's Got Talent* and *American Idol* were all the rage. Because they were so unbelievably popular, many of my musical friends believed landing a spot on one of those stages would be their fast track to a sustainable career in the arts. Some even made it, and while I was incredibly proud of them (and thrilled to see their talent recognized), it rarely played out the way they'd hoped.

Just as a viral TikTok hit rarely leads to a long-term career, TV exposure tends to be a flash in the pan. It burns bright for a moment, but very rarely generates the kind of lasting warmth needed for an actual career. As I shared in the previous chapter, art is about more than transactions; it's about relationship. TV is great for the kind of relationship that might be akin to a one-night stand, but as anyone in a long-term, committed relationship knows, meaningful bonds take presence, effort, and consistency to build.

This is where Kevin Kelly's concept of "1,000 True Fans" comes in. His idea is simple, yet profound: if 1,000 people truly love what you do and each pays $100 a year to support your work, you've got a $100,000 career. True fans are your insurance policy against financial failure.

The catch with this concept is that it takes time to generate *true* fans. Unlike casual followers, true fans are people who know you and you know *them*.

The ones who are going to support your Patreon, buy everything you put out, and show up to your events are going to be the people that you take the time to speak with, share your life with, and create for. This kind of loyalty can't be rushed. That means that unlike the often overhyped promises of talent shows, record label deals, contests, booking agents, and social media algorithms, you're going to have to work hard at relationship-building. In this context, zagging likely means intentionally slowing down and building something real with your audience. Again, I'll quote my friend, Jeff Goins: "The Starving Artist waits to be noticed. The Thriving Artist cultivates patrons."[13]

When it comes to cultivating patrons, it may help to think of yourself less like a performer up on a stage and more like the host of a dinner party. You're curating an experience, inviting people into your world, making space for conversation, connection, and meaning. This kind of intentionality brings about something sacred: it turns passive consumers into loyal supporters.

When your supporters see you wrestle with your craft, take risks, and put yourself out there, they feel like they're part of the journey. When you win, they win. When you stumble, they're there to lift you up—just as you've lifted them with your art. In time, your story becomes part of their own.

Art has always thrived in the context of relational community because it's only in this context where both creatives and broader society benefits. Communities nurture artists, and artists serve communities. You cannot remove one from the other without serious consequences.

In a speech given in honor of the poet Robert Frost, US President John F. Kennedy rightly asserted that art nourishes the roots of culture by stating:

> But democratic society—in it, the highest duty of the writer, the composer, the artist is to remain true to himself and to let the chips fall where they may. In serving his vision of the truth, the artist best serves his nation. And the nation which disdains the mission of art invites the fate of Robert Frost's hired man, the fate of having "nothing to look backward to with pride, and nothing to look forward to with hope."[14]

Meanwhile, AI is fundamentally *asocial*, created without the feedback loops, friction, and fellowship that has always driven great art—and great societies—forward. AI is a mirror, selling us back to ourselves, only increasing our isolation. That's exactly why today's artists must invite communal interaction. Whether through live performance, participatory art, community storytelling, or some form of collaborative creation, the most resilient artists will be those who build moments that cannot so easily be duplicated by code. They understand that the creative life is a dialogue, not a monologue.

This goes against many creatives' natural inclinations. Many of us (myself included) like to create in isolation because it's therapeutic. We tend to be a bit more introverted and sometimes withdraw from the world rather than press in. This needn't be seen as a bad thing! Often, our introversion is part of our superpower, allowing us to think deeply and give voice to that which often goes unsaid. But if we ever expect to move from hobbyist to professional, pursuing community is unequivocally essential.

The good news is, if you're niching down—like we talked about in the previous chapter—your people will start to appear. The key is to recognize them when they're standing in front of you and intentionally step into relationship with them. Please note: once you begin building those relationships, it will be crucial not to rely on rented land to maintain connection. What do I mean by that? Well, let's just say I once had a fantastic following on a little platform called MySpace. And then, just like that, the entire platform vanished. When you build your career primarily on someone else's platform, you're renting space on land you don't own. Algorithms change. CEOs pivot. Entire networks vanish.

Smart artists build their own ecosystems—email/text lists, gated online communities, local gatherings. These are places where connection isn't so easily filtered through someone else's financial interests. That doesn't mean you have to abandon social platforms altogether. But it does mean letting go of the myth of an algorithm granting you the wish of a viable career. In exchange for releasing the fantasy of overnight superstardom—a world without the messiness of real, symbiotic relationship—you gain something far more realistic and sustainable: a community of people who love, support, and believe in you. Not because you're trending, but because you actually mean something to them.

If I'm starting to sound like old-man-yelling-at-cloud, I get it. The truth, however, is that I've spent my entire life living at the intersection of creativity and technology. Camping out there has expanded my imagination, sparked moments of absolute magic, and helped me build a lasting career. I just don't believe that the current iteration of the tech industry always has our best interests at heart, especially when it comes to our mental health.

The Burnout Economy and the Art of Saying "No"

In a 2017 interview, Sean Parker—one of the early leaders of Facebook—admitted that the goal of Facebook's and Instagram's founders was to create "a social-validation feedback loop . . . exactly the kind of thing that a hacker like myself would come up with, because you're exploiting a vulnerability in human psychology."[15] They did a great job.

Flash forward to 2025: the British Standards Institution surveyed 1,293 young people between the ages of sixteen and twenty-one. Of those surveyed, 68 percent said that they felt the time they spent online was detrimental to their mental health, almost 70 percent feel worse after using social media, and 46 percent said that they would rather be young in a world without the internet altogether.[16] Statistics like this reveal a growing chorus of intergenerational disillusionment. To quote technology writer and podcaster Ed Zitron: "I actually believe that there is a consumer awakening happening against the tech industry. Not because the tech industry as an idea is bad, but because what the tech industry has become is so vile and so antithetical to what Silicon Valley was built on and the reasons that we use tech to connect and empower human beings."[17] Whether you call it a movement toward "slow tech" or simply a cultural correction, we're seeing a surprising revival of what can only be described as modern-day Luddism.

Historically, Luddism referred to a social movement of English textile workers in the early nineteenth century who protested the introduction of new machinery by destroying it. It's important to note that the Luddites were not against technology itself, but against the specific ways it was used to exploit workers and concentrate power and wealth in the hands of a few. While the original movement was a protest against threats to the people's livelihoods, the term is also used today to describe a modern opposition to certain technologies, especially those tied to automation, surveillance, and digital overreach.

In his book *Blood in the Machine: The Origins of the Rebellion Against Big Tech*, tech journalist Brian Merchant writes, "The history of the Luddites—the real ones, not the pejorative figment of the entrepreneurial imagination—gives us a framework to evaluate the utility of technologies and their social impacts. Erasing that history collapses our thinking about how tech and automation affect our working lives—and the choices we have to address the disruption they bring."[18] This framework for resistance applies not just to labor politics, but to creative practice. Zagging toward friction and cultivating true fans can be a powerful way to resist the burnout economy and reclaim the invisible rhythms of creativity. Those rhythms are essential yet often overlooked in our productivity-obsessed culture.

In one of my favorite books on creativity, *Orbiting the Giant Hairball*, artist Gordon MacKenzie likened the creative process to one of a cow making milk. When observed, only a small part of a cow making milk can actually be seen. We can see a cow that cows eat grass, and we can see the cow being milked when it's hooked up to the machine. But the actual process of milk creation is invisible. If you wanted to maximize productivity, you might find it prudent to try and milk the cow twenty-four seven, but that wouldn't produce more milk. It would kill the cow.

The same is true when we treat our creativity as "content." CEOs and product evangelists from every social media and digital distribution platform have been pushing the same agenda to creatives: *upload, upload, upload*. These platforms have expressed the importance of consistent content, regardless of quality. While there is some level of truth in these claims (creators, like anyone else, do need to be disciplined and consistent in their marketing), let's also be clear: the ones who truly benefit from that hamster wheel of performance are the platforms themselves. Every new video, song, and post adds to their addictive feeds, keeping people scrolling longer, which translates into higher ad rates. It's an extraction economy, and creatives have been the resource.

The pressure to be constantly visible, endlessly productive, and algorithmically optimized is not a creative strategy; it's a recipe for becoming a modern-day John Henry, working yourself to death. Sure, maybe you'll "win," but at what cost?

Fellow creative, you do not have to participate in that crazymaking. Many will insist that if you want a viable creative career, you do, but you don't. Lest we forget: we are called to be artists, not "influencers" or "content creators." All those titles really mean is that you are, as Simon Sinek bluntly puts it, a "freelance employee of an algorithm."[19] If you believe you can play that game and remain emotionally resilient, great! But over the long haul, the data is simply not in your favor.

In the first comprehensive study on creator mental health, Creators 4 Mental Health found that only 8 percent of self-described content creators described their mental health as "excellent."[20] For those who have been creating for more than five years, that number drops to 4 percent. The same report revealed that 65 percent experience anxiety or depression related to their work, and 62 percent feel burned out. In short: the longer someone stays on the hamster wheel, the worse their mental health becomes.

If you want to promote on platforms that monetize an attention economy, do it wisely. Be intentional, set limits, and make sure the effort serves your goals. Consider:

- Creating routines and systems that make your work easily manageable:
  - Designate a space and workflow to easily set up and record content.
  - Batch-create content to relieve the pressure of daily posting.
  - Utilize scheduling and management tools like Hootsuite, Buffer, FeedHive, etc.
- Shifting from "producing" to "documenting." Authentic, behind-the-scenes content generally garners just as high of levels of engagement as highly polished pieces.
- Prioritizing meaningful engagement over vanity metrics such as "likes" or "followers."
- Taking recurring breaks for walking, exercise, meditation, breath work, etc.
- Protecting yourself from trolls and negative comments by refusing to engage with negative or hateful comments.

Staying Grounded

Artists who go the distance take whatever steps necessary to protect against burnout. In his seminal work, *A Failure of Nerve: Leadership in the Age of the Quick Fix*, leadership consultant and family therapist Dr. Edwin Friedman stated, "Any renaissance . . . depends primarily not only on new data and techniques, but on the capacity of leaders to separate themselves from the surrounding emotional climate so that they can break through the barriers that are keeping everyone from 'going the other way.'"[21] What Friedman is describing is self-differentiation: the ability to remain rooted in your own identity and values rather than being swept up in other people's anxieties or expectations. For creatives, part of this means refusing to let anyone or anything dictate your worth or your pace. This means that you don't need to be afraid of taking intentional sabbaticals from platforms and activities that suck the life and joy out of your work. Contrary to what anyone says, there is absolutely nothing wrong with setting boundaries around your availability, time, and energy. You do not have to be all things to all people.

This runs directly counter to what most of us are told. When you zag toward wellness though, you live out of the fullness of who you truly are and give others permission to do the same. Parker J. Palmer puts it beautifully in *Let Your Life Speak*: "Self-care is never a selfish act—it is simply good stewardship of the only gift I have, the gift I was put on earth to offer to others. Anytime we can listen to true self and give it the care it requires, we do so not only for ourselves but for the many others whose lives we touch."[22] Choosing this course might mean you never "go viral" or end up on any popular, competitive TV shows. Was that really what got you into creating in the first place though?

In order to actually have something to say in our work, artists must be self-differentiated enough to know who they are and why they create. In his book, *Ten Arguments for Deleting Your Social Media Accounts Right Now*, Silicon Valley pioneer, Jaron Lanier, considers this when he asks: "What if listening to an inner voice or heeding a passion for ethics or beauty were to lead to more important work in the long term, even if it measured as less successful in the moment? What if deeply reaching a small number of people matters more than reaching everybody with nothing?"[23]

This is the essence of zagging toward friction, slowly cultivating true fans, and honoring the rhythms of creativity. It's prioritizing your craft more than your "influence." It's caring more for your supporters than the algorithm. And it's choosing to go down a path that allows you to do your art consistently, sustainably, and authentically (warts and all) over the long haul.

Your Turn

As we close this chapter, now's the time to pause, reflect, and begin putting some of these ideas into practice. These questions and exercises are designed to help you deepen your creative identity, sharpen your voice, and begin cultivating the kind of originality no machine can touch.

Questions

1 Where in your creative life have you been chasing speed or scale at the expense of depth or meaning?

2 Where have you recently said "yes" to something(s) that drain you? What would saying "no" make space for?

3 Where in your life have you seen friction be a *good* thing?

Exercises

1 Reach Out to Five True Fans:
Identify five people who consistently support your work. Send each a personal message or gift. Ask them what they love most about your work and what they'd love to see more of.

2 Map Your Ecosystem:
Create a visual map of your current audience touchpoints (social media, email list, live events, Substack, etc.). Highlight which ones you own and which ones are rented. Then, brainstorm ways to draw people over to the ones you own.

3 Design a Friction-Based Experience:
Develop a creative offering that intentionally includes friction. This could be a limited-edition drop, a password-protected page, or a live event with no phones allowed, or a puzzle that fans must solve to access your work.

Notes

1 Lanier, Jaron. *Ten Arguments for Deleting Your Social Media Accounts Right Now*. Henry Holt and Company, 2018.

2 Dredge, Stuart. "Spotify CEO Talks Covid-19, Artist Incomes and Podcasting (Interview)." *Music Ally*, July 30, 2020. Accessed December 17, 2025. https://musically.com/2020/07/30/spotify-daniel-ek-interview/.

3 Spotify has been accused many times of gaming the system with their own generative AI slop filling up playlists like Indie Chill Mix and Jazz in the Background. Investigative author Liz Pelly writes extensively on this in her book *Mood Machine: The Rise of Spotify and the Costs of the Perfect Playlist*.

4 Licensing International. "Slipstream and WexWorks Media Team Up to Commercialize Viral Hit 'Funny Song,' Touting More than 42 Billion Social Media Views." *Licensing International*, June 30, 2025. Accessed December 17, 2025. https://licensinginternational.org/news/slipstream-and-wexworks-media-team-up-to-commercialize-viral-hit-funny-song-touting-more-than-42-billion-social-media-views/.

5 Peterson, Arabella. "What Happens When Your Song Goes Viral on TikTok? We Speak to the Most Listened-to Artists You've Never Heard Of." *Whynow*, February 8, 2023. Accessed December 17, 2025. https://whynow.co.uk/read/most-viral-tik-tok-songs.

6 For a sobering analysis of the business and cultural impact of social media on its primary market—teenagers—I highly recommend reading *The Anxious Generation* by New York University sociologist Jonathan Haidt.

7 Mulligan, Mark, Kahlert, Hanna, Thakrar, Kriss, Cirisano, Tatiana and Jones, Oliviaet al. *All Eyes, No Ears: Why Virality Is Not Building Fandom*. MIDiA Research, September 2025.

8 Mundaden, Maria. "2025 Social Media Industry Benchmark Report." *RivalIQ*, February 25, 2025. Accessed December 17, 2025. https://www.rivaliq.com/blog/social-media-industry-benchmark-report/.

9 mekusum. "'In Rainbows': The Radiohead Album Thom Yorke Said Made More Money Than Any Other." *Rock Music World*, October 30, 2025. Accessed December 17, 2025. https://rockmusicworld.net/in-rainbows-the-radiohead-album-thom-yorke-said-made-more-money-than-any-other/.

10 American Psychological Association. "Effort Justification." *APA Dictionary of Psychology*, April 19, 2018. Accessed December 17, 2025. https://dictionary.apa.org/effort-justification.

11 Healey, Eugene (eugbrandtrat). "Friction Is What's Missing When Designing Meaningful Experiences." *Instagram*, August 25, 2025. Accessed December 17, 2025. https://www.instagram.com/reel/DNzBSt74guZ/.

12 Lest we forget the concepts discussed in Chapter 7, "Craft Is the New Creative Currency," if you ask your audience to walk toward you, there better be something at the end that's worth the journey.

13 Goins, Jeff. *Real Artists Don't Starve: Timeless Strategies for Thriving in the New Creative Age*. Nelson Books, 2017.

14 Kennedy, John F. "Remarks at Amherst College, Amherst, Massachusetts, October 26, 1963." Speech, Amherst, MA, October 26, 1963. John F. Kennedy Presidential Library and Museum. https://www.jfklibrary.org/archives/other-resources/john-f-kennedy-speeches/amherst-college-19631026.

15 Solon, Olivia. "Ex-Facebook President Sean Parker: Site Made to Exploit Human 'Vulnerability.'" *The Guardian*, November 9, 2017. Accessed December 17, 2025. https://www.theguardian.com/technology/2017/nov/09/facebook-sean-parker-vulnerability-brain-psychology.

16 British Standards Institution. *Cross-brand NSS DT MPD MP COPOLCO 0525 Brochure*. White paper. May 2025. Accessed December 17, 2025. https://www.bsigroup.com/siteassets/pdf/en/insights-and-media/insights/white-papers/gl-grp-cross-brand-nss-dt-mpd-mp-copolco-0525-broc.pdf.

17 Conover, Adam. *The AI Hoax Is Destroying America with Ed Zitron*. YouTube video, 1:40:05. Posted February 26, 2025. Accessed December 17, 2025. https://www.youtube.com/watch?v=wAUTbQ4rPI4.

18 Merchant, Brian. *Blood in the Machine: The Origins of the Rebellion Against Big Tech*. Little, Brown, 2023.

19 The Diary of A CEO. *Simon Sinek: You're Being Lied to About AI's Real Purpose! We're Teaching Our Kids To Not Be Human!*. YouTube video, 2:06:15. Posted May 26, 2025. Accessed December 17, 2025. https://www.youtube.com/watch?v=W4tqbEmplug.

20 Creators 4 Mental Health. "The Content Creator Mental Health Study." *Creators 4 Mental Health*, 2024. https://www.creators4mentalhealth.com/study.

21 Friedman, Edwin H. *A Failure of Nerve: Leadership in the Age of the Quick Fix*. Revised ed. Church Publishing, 2017.

22 Palmer, Parker J. *Let Your Life Speak: Listening for the Voice of Vocation*. Jossey-Bass, 2000.

23 Lanier, Jaron. *Ten Arguments for Deleting Your Social Media Accounts Right Now*. Henry Holt and Company, 2018.

10 Keeping the Channel Open

Cultural movements, hard to define and lacking clear boundaries, are typically labeled in retrospect. At the risk of making a premature claim, I offer that we may be witnessing a new Romantic resistance to a current disenchantment. Once again, art, aesthetics, and nature might be critical ingredients for countering this modern malady.[1]

NEUROSCIENTIST DR. ANJAN CHATTERJEE

Congratulations. Not only have you made it to the last chapter of the book, but by even getting this far you've embodied a powerful biological truth: that you are capable of transforming your fear, anger, and/or pessimism into an opportunity to learn, grow, and adapt. You've effectively rebelled against the voice of stagnation and defeat that says, "dead end." Lest you think I'm pandering, I assure you, I am not. I'll unpack this more in a moment . . .

By this point, perhaps you can tell that I'm not all that impressed with most of today's dominant generative AI systems. While what we're seeing certainly has its uses, set against the media's relentless fixation with boomers, doomers, and their exaggerated narratives, I have yet to encounter anything truly remarkable.[2] Overall, I tend to agree with journalist Ross Barkan:

> Much of the flickering reality of (generative AI's) presence in our world is that it is performing tasks that have been the province of human beings for many thousands of years. We can already read, write, and create. We can paint. We can publish books. We can make music. What is the purpose of having a machine do it for us? *Why?*[3]

Frankly, I might be more impressed by these things if they weren't being mandatorily foisted upon us in every area of our online lives, dragging behind them a multi-headed corpse of environmental destruction, IP theft, exploitative labor, and an impending economic blowback.

Ultimately, what I see in these technologies are some interesting plug-ins (a piece of software that "plugs in" to an existing application) that people might elect to use when needing to come up with different ideas. Outside of some new ways to search and perform perfunctory tasks like emailing, generative AI has yet to produce anything substantiative. Sure, it's slopped out novel videos of SpongeBob getting pulled over by a police officer and remixed tracks of what Iron Maiden's *Powerslave* album might have sounded like as a funk project, but that's about it. Instead, we have survey after survey revealing that 95 percent of generative AI pilot projects fail to deliver meaningful value,[4] 88 percent of undergraduate students are using it to cheat,[5] and rather than ushering in promised financial, medical, and environmental miracles, we're inheriting new economic, physical, and ecological burdens from the sprawling datacenters rising in our backyards.[6] As part of what Canadian-British author Cory Doctorow calls "enshittification,"[7] this current wave of AI seems mostly dedicated to making everything online worse. Much worse.

A recent analysis suggested that AI-generated content now accounts for over half of all new written material on the internet.[8] While this estimate only focuses on written content, many warn that the true proportion of AI-generated material (e.g., images, videos, audio, and text) is likely even higher. There are also concerns about feedback loops, where AI models are now training on AI-generated data, degrading overall content quality each time models retrain. It's like a mathematically complex version of photocopying an image over and over, except that in this case, the original image was unnecessarily pixelated to begin with.

Meanwhile, despite so much talk of AI someday being able to replace creatives, study after study finds both deployers and consumers disappointed. Case in point: in late 2025, researchers from the *Center for AI Safety* collected 240 creative freelance projects. These were real projects that humans got paid for: video editing, architecture design, 3D modeling, mini-game development, etc. They then employed AI agents from ChatGPT 5, Claude 4.5, and Grok 4 (you know, the same systems that supposedly passed the bar exam and various medical licensing assessments) to perform these jobs. In short, their performance was a disaster.

Out of the $144,000 worth of projects, the best the bots earned was $1,700. They successfully completed only 2.5 percent of the work—failing a staggering

97 percent of the time. When the researchers looked at why the systems failed, they found patterns of gross incompetence: stick-figure sketches passed off as professional graphics, 3D buildings warped from every angle, eight-second videos for projects demanding eight minutes, and voiceovers so robotic they sounded like bad sci-fi. Nearly half of the outputs were so bad, they wouldn't survive a high school project review.[9]

Bottom line? Give the bots real, economically viable work, and you get 2.5 percent success and 97 percent embarrassment.

So, no, as of this writing, I'm not that impressed. Furthermore, I'm not fearful and neither should you be. This isn't to say that there isn't cause for concern, but what we need right now is levelheadedness—remaining vigilant, resisting the allure of hype, and fighting for what is good, just, and true. Behind the AI media frenzy are million-dollar PR firms shoveling propaganda into our feeds every day. Frankly, they've done a much better job at promoting this stuff than the tech companies have done with actually building it. It's like we're living through a satirical take on that Jurassic Park line: "your scientists were so obsessed with whether they *should* do this, they never stopped to ask whether they *could*."

Like every other AI summer, this current season of hype and investment cannot, and as a result, will not, last. Stein's Law states: "If something cannot go on forever, it will stop."[10] Coined by macro and political economist Herbert Stein, it's a maxim that states that trends—whether in economic growth, government debt, or any other area—will eventually end when they become unsustainable. This is what happened with the other AI winters and right now, you don't have to be an economist to see that the expense-to-income ratio of these synthetic systems is completely unsustainable.[11]

Every user these platforms gain, the more money they lose. Every time they turn on another GPU (i.e., graphics processing units, most of which are currently provided by Nvidia), the more money they lose. Every time they release a more advanced model that chews through more tokens, the more money they lose.[12] At some point, AI is going to fall dormant again and the inevitability of another winter will be upon us.

This isn't to say that AI is going away. Even when the big tech bets crash and burn, remnants of these systems will remain. Much of it will get embedded into everyday tools like the "find" feature in a Word doc. Meanwhile, others will build better, cheaper AI tools once all those premium GPUs currently leased to today's datacenters flood the secondhand market for pennies on the dollar.[13] As a result, let's look to the future with some overarching principles that empower creativity and growth, no matter what tomorrow brings.

Growth Mindset

As I was saying at the start of the chapter: congratulations. By reaching this point in the book, you're already demonstrating resilience, perseverance, and what award-winning Stanford psychologist Dr. Carol Dweck calls a "growth mindset." Educators talk about growth mindset all the time because it represents one of the most influential neurological insights in the field of teaching. At its core, a growth mindset is the belief that abilities, intelligence, and talents are not static, and can be developed through effort, curiosity, and a willingness to learn. People who live out of this mindset embrace challenges, persist through setbacks, and see critical feedback as fuel for improvement. As Dweck puts it: "People in a growth mindset don't just seek challenge, they thrive on it."[14]

Contrast that with a fixed mindset: "In a fixed mindset, people believe their basic qualities, like their intelligence or talent, are simply fixed traits."[15] Those operating from this perspective often avoid challenges, give up easily when obstacles arise, and view effort as pointless, believing that failure is a reflection of a lack of innate ability. Put in other terms: they live from a scarcity worldview versus an abundance worldview.

Far from mere pop psychology, Dweck's conclusions rest on decades of research that consistently demonstrates how people with a growth mindset tend to be more resilient, creative, and successful.[16] In *Mindset: The New Psychology of Success*, she writes: "The passion for stretching yourself and sticking to it, even (or especially) when it's not going well, is the hallmark of the growth mindset. This is the mindset that allows people to thrive during some of the most challenging times in their lives."[17]

While the difference between a growth mindset and a fixed mindset often marks the line between failure and success, Dweck says it can come down to one word: *yet*. For example: "I don't understand . . . yet" or "I can't do this . . . yet." You can probably see now why most educators (especially in K–12 environments) are so passionate to share Dweck's research with their students. In her 2014 TED Talk, *The Power of Believing You Can Improve*, Dweck explained:

> In study after study, [individuals operating out of a fixed mindset] run from difficulty. Scientists measured the electrical activity from the brain as students confronted an error. On the left, you see the fixed mindset students. There's hardly any activity. They run from the error. They don't engage with it. But on the right, you have the students with the growth mindset, the idea that abilities can be developed. They engage deeply. Their brain is on fire with *yet*.[18]

In times of disruption, the power of *yet* may be one of the most critical determinants of success—not just for students, but for anyone. In practice, *yet* means embracing lifelong learning and being adaptable when the ground beneath starts to shift. I truly believe, based on the data of current scientific research, that what truly differentiates high-performing, resilient individuals from those who fall by the wayside, may well be their capacity for growth. In sum: people who live with a growth mindset are people who are antifragile. They're "AI-proof."

Artificial intelligence excels at pattern recognition, speed, and processing vast amounts of data, but it struggles with the qualities that define human adaptability: curiosity, resilience, and creative problem-solving. A growth mindset embodies these traits. Sure, those who live out this conviction may still feel frustrated by change, but they also see it as an opportunity.[19]

Studies on neuroplasticity—the capacity of the brain to develop and change throughout life—show that the brain can literally rewire itself in response to challenge and failure.[20] This means individuals who embrace learning can perpetually acquire new skills, pivot into new opportunities, and fearlessly innovate. As Dweck reminds us: "Becoming is better than being,"[21] emphasizing that malleability is a lifelong process, not a fixed state.

When this gets internalized, something shifts and people begin to find gratitude in failures, challenges, and setbacks. "I'm glad I was fired; I never would have founded my own design firm." "I'm grateful my discipline is being turned upside down; we've been overdue for a creative renaissance." "I'm thankful the software I relied on was discontinued; I've been needing to learn a new approach anyways."

Obviously, this kind of mindset doesn't come naturally. Just like any other muscle, mental effort can be painful. But it's also essential for growth and developing new skills. We humans instinctively avoid discomfort. Our brains are hardwired to prioritize fear, negativity, and frustration over positivity. Psychologists call this a "negativity bias."[22]

In a 2023 study, researchers found that negative experiences tend to stick to the brain like Velcro, quickly encoded into emotional memory. Positive experiences, by contrast, require sustained attention (typically ten to twenty seconds) to transfer into long-term memory. Otherwise, they "slide off" like Teflon.[23] This bias stems from our survival instincts: missing a threat could be fatal, while missing a reward is typically far less consequential.

Negativity bias may have helped our ancestors survive, but in today's fast-changing world, that instinct can hold us back. What's more helpful now is cultivating a positivity bias—a mindset that looks for possibility instead of threat. Again, this doesn't diminish threats; it simply puts them in proper perspective. Times of challenge need not be feared. Setbacks need not have the final word. Becoming is better than being.

If it's hard to believe in the validity of statements like these, I can empathize. While I tend to be an optimist by nature, I too can get overwhelmed by a relentlessly shifting landscape that consistently echoes threats of automation. This is why—especially in times of disruption—the ability to reshape how we think may be the most creative tool we have.

The Tools Do Not = Creativity

In his book *Creativity: Flow and the Psychology of Discovery and Invention*, the late Hungarian-American psychologist Mihaly Csikszentmihalyi offered this incisive insight: "Creative individuals are remarkable for their ability to adapt to almost any situation and to make do with whatever is at hand to reach their goals."[24] It's a generous compliment to anyone who has had a dream, but not the resources. Unfortunately, working creatives often confuse their tools with their art. But tools are not art. They never were and they never will be. Tools are a means to an end.

No one ever enrolled in college to major in "pencil." Likewise, 3D animators don't earn degrees in "Maya" or "Blender." Tools exist to help us turn ideas into finished work, but they're just that—tools. There are always multiple paths to the same destination.

Do you remember that twelve-song album I talked about at the beginning of Chapter 1? I created that on a Roland VS-880. If you've never heard of it, I wouldn't blame you. That piece of hardware hasn't been relevant since the early 2000s. The world moved on, mostly leaving behind dedicated digital hardware devices for software-based solutions. But back then, I spent a *lot* of time learning the ins and outs of that gray box.

As digital recording evolved, so did I. My first step away from dedicated hardware was a desktop computer running Magix Music Maker—an affordable, entry-level program that gave me so much more freedom than the Roland. Things that used to take hours performing on the tiny, black-and-white LCD screen of that hardware recorder could now be done in a few mouse clicks, fully visible on a color computer monitor. Because of a new tool, I could now focus more on actually *creating* than fiddling with editing and tweaking.

Over time, I made another switch to a program called Sonar. It wasn't cheap, but as I was beginning to be paid for my work, I knew I needed to own a tool that allowed me to do things even more efficiently and with a higher degree of excellence. For years, Sonar and I worked well together. I loved it and frankly, wasn't planning on changing platforms ever again. But as my network grew, I kept hitting the same wall: all the industry professionals I was increasingly collaborating with were using something called Pro Tools. Exporting sessions for them meant jumping through hoops to make files compatible. Eventually, I realized I had to yet again switch to another tool.

Unlike Music Maker and Sonar, Pro Tools was built for much more than music. It's also used for sound design, audio post-production in film and television, and dominates most broadcast environments. Unfortunately, that versatility came at a cost: proprietary hardware, complex routing, endless keyboard shortcuts, and customization overload. When I first switched, every time I opened the program I felt like a beginner again. It was frustrating. But I knew that if I was going to have a viable career, I was going to have to brute force my way through learning it.

Fast forward fifteen years and Pro Tools is second nature to me. Along the way, I've learned other software like Ableton Live, Logic, FMOD, and Finale. Each of these programs have their quirks and learning curve. But learning each tool has made me a much better musician, producer, and teacher. My creative skill set has considerably grown—not because I mastered the specific buttons and menus of each app, but because each tool has taught me deeper principles of my craft.

What truly sets creative professionals apart isn't mastery of a single tool, be it a pencil, program, plug-in, or instrument. It's their ability to solve problems, create never-before-experienced beauty, defamiliarize the mundane, and awaken the imagination. That's what primarily separates the creative arts from the performing arts.

Performers are hired to reproduce Bach, Arthur Miller, or Martha Graham. There's nothing wrong with that; this can be just as equally profound! But there is a marked difference between interpretation and invention, recreation versus creativity. I know brilliant pianists who have never even attempted improvisation or composition. I also know brilliant producers who can't play a note. Mastery of a tool is valuable, but it's not the same as mastery of creativity.

Like it or not, the toolbox of the working creative is going to evolve. As innovation accelerates, we will likely see new ways of getting to quality solutions faster. This can be frustrating. After all, we spend so much time learning how to get the job done with our hammers and shovels. But life moves on. Tools change. Creativity tends to follow techno-innovation.

The good news is that the principles and fundamentals behind our tools always remain. Just as learning foundational programming languages like BASIC or C+ teaches coders concepts that carry over to modern languages like Python or C#, every discipline rests on core principles that outlast the tools. Mastery of color theory still shapes our perception of contrast and balance, just as knowing major and minor scales still unlocks melodic potential on a laptop. If you find yourself frustrated because the tides are changing, take heart—nothing is wasted.

When AI-assisted tools become commonplace, technical know-how will still matter, but the real edge will fall to the creative professionals who understand the bigger picture. At its core, aesthetics is the philosophical study of beauty, art, and taste. It asks how we experience and judge these qualities in both art and nature, and how sensory perception, cultural background, and personal sensitivity shape our sense of what is beautiful or moving. Some principles are universal—contrast and harmony, organic unity, distillation—while others are discipline-specific.

As our tools evolve, a growth mindset not only embraces the challenge of learning something new, but it also recognizes that tools are ultimately just a means to an end. Creativity is about grasping the human condition, telling stories that move people, and understanding why certain forms of expression resonate in specific contexts. Mastering today's tools is important, but it's the deeper principles of aesthetics that equip us to navigate and transcend whatever resources and technologies are at hand.

The Priority of Purpose

Like many creatives, I tend to get bored when I'm forced to do the same thing over and over. As a result, I tend to like change. I like learning new instruments, new approaches, and new techniques. But the current season of innovation can, at times, leave me reeling. Keeping up with it all can feel like chasing a horizon that never stops moving.

The beauty of the growth mindset is that it doesn't demand we instantly comprehend every new tool or trend. Instead, it invites us to face each shift with curiosity, patience, and the sturdy confidence that regardless of whatever comes next, we can learn. We may not understand . . . yet. But we will.

As AI continues to evolve, a growth mindset teaches us that disruption need not all be a bad thing. In *Man's Search for Meaning*, Victor Frankl reminded us: "Life is never made unbearable by circumstances, but only by lack of meaning and purpose."[25] Frankl wrote these words shortly after enduring the horrors of Nazi concentration camps, proving that meaning, not circumstances, is what makes life bearable. If purpose can sustain a human spirit through that level of darkness, imagine what it can do for us as we navigate the changes affecting our disciplines. This is precisely why understanding your *why* is so important.

Merriam-Webster defines "purpose" as:

a) the reason something is done or used,

b) the feeling of being determined to do or achieve something,

c) the aim or goal of a person.[26]

Those are helpful definitions, but what is *yours*? Beyond art being personally fulfilling, can you articulate the deeper thread that compels you to make? Why are you an artist? Or as the poet Mary Oliver so exquisitely asked in *The Summer Day*: "Tell me, what is it you plan to do with your one wild and precious life?"[27]

However you answer that question, I encourage you to write it down. Form it out, word-for-word and when you're done, put it somewhere visible. Purpose becomes a lifeline when we're overwhelmed, discouraged, or doubting our path. No tool, no amount of money, no degree or public accolade can replace the anchoring force of purpose. It brings life to grief, hope to despair, and movement to stagnation. When your purpose is clear, you can return to it, rehearse it, and rebuild yourself upon it.

Whatever your *why* is, I implore you: don't let anything steal the joy of creating. It is the sickness and the cure all rolled up into one. It's why you began in your craft, and it's what will carry you long after the storm passes. Sometimes we need to remind ourselves of this. I like the way Derek Sivers put it:

> Here's how to live: create.
>
> The most valuable real estate in the world is the graveyard.
>
> There lie millions of half-written books, ideas never launched, and talents never developed. Most people die with everything still inside of them . . .
>
> Let the deadline of death drive you.
>
> Create until your last breath.
>
> Let your last spark of life go into your work.
>
> Die empty, so death takes only a corpse.[28]

Fellow creative, do not fear this moment . . . nor any moment. Yes, fight for what is yours. Stand up for your ideas, labor, and value. But do not cower or flinch back in fear, letting the world silence the beauty that is within. We need you. Perhaps now more than ever, we need you.

We need your craft, inspiring awe in us with your genius in communication. We need your humanity, tethering us to something deeper than our small, scattered selves. We need your quirkiness, awkwardness, and sharp edges, challenging us and showing us how to see and hear the world differently. We need your passion and innovation, giving us better ways to think and live. And we need your creativity, reminding us of how unbelievably amazing the gift of life truly is.

The age of AI is not the first time technology has unsettled the creative world, and it will not be the last. This is just another point in history where innovation brings about disruption. That can be scary. It can feel threatening. But as the revolutionary American dancer and choreographer Martha Graham once said:

> There is only one of you in all time, this expression is unique, and if you block it, it will never exist through any other medium; and be lost. The world will not have it. It is not your business to determine how good it is, not how it compares with other expression. It is your business to keep it yours clearly and directly, to keep the channel open. You do not even have to believe in yourself or your work. You have to keep open and aware directly to the urges that motivate you. Keep the channel open.[29]

Keep the channel open. No matter what the present holds or the future may bring, may you live life courageously, offering every last spark of your creative fire. When your time is done, may fear not have the last word, but a body and legacy of artistic brilliance that shone in seasons of light and seasons of darkness alike.

Your Turn

As we close this chapter, now's the time to pause, reflect, and begin putting some of these ideas into practice. These questions and exercises are designed to help you deepen your creative identity, sharpen your voice, and begin cultivating the kind of originality no machine can touch.

Questions

1 Where in your creative life do you most feel the pull toward a fixed mindset? How might adding the word *yet* shift that narrative?

2 Think about a recent setback or disappointment in your creative work. In what ways might this be an invitation to learn, adapt, or grow?

3 What legacy of creativity do you hope to leave behind? What fears, habits, or assumptions currently stand in the way?

Exercises

1 Your Purpose Statement:
Write a concise, vivid 1–2 sentence creative mission statement that captures why you make art. It may be helpful to start by first imagining your creative purpose and noting what words or images immediately surface. Even more potent, see if you can articulate where, in Frederick Buechner words, "your deep gladness and the world's deep hunger meet."[30]

2 Negative Bias Flip:
For the next week, start each day by writing down at least one creative opportunity in front of you. Look for encouraging entrepreneurial opportunities and allow your brain to practice noticing what usually slides off.

3 Your "Die Empty" List:
Taking inspiration from the Sivers quote, list three ideas, projects, or dreams you don't want to die with. Circle one and take a concrete step toward making a reality.

Notes

1 Chatterjee, Anjan. "The New Romantics." *Psychology Today*, March 15, 2024. Accessed December 19, 2025. https://www.psychologytoday.com/us/blog/brain-behavior-and-beauty/202403/the-new-romantics.

2 I should note that I am not referring to *all* AI, but this season's generative variety. For example, I see tremendous promise in traditional/predictive AI in fields such as medicine, where systems can be utilized to examine existing datasets for diagnostic insights or risk prediction. To help illustrate the difference: Google's *Med-Gemini* (i.e., a generative LLM) was caught red-handed in August 2025 for hallucinating a nonexistent part of the brain. Basically, in one of the initial research papers where Google tried to show off the capacities of their med-specific LLM, the model referenced the "basilar ganglia": a part of the brain that doesn't exist. Obviously, this does not impress—nor surprise—me. Hayden Field at *The Verge* was the first to report on this. Her article can be found here: https://www.theverge.com/health/718049/google-med-gemini-basilar-ganglia-paper-typo-hallucination.

3 Barkan, Ross. "The Rise of the New Romanticism." *Ross Barkan*, February 20, 2025. Accessed December 2, 2025. https://rosselliotbarkan.com/p/the-rise-of-the-new-romanticism.

4 Challapally, Aditya, Pease, Chris, Raskar, Ramesh, and Chari, Pradyumna. *The GenAI Divide: State of AI in Business 2025*. MIT NANDA, July 2025. Accessed December 3, 2025. https://mlq.ai/media/quarterly_decks/v0.1_State_of_AI_in_Business_2025_Report.pdf.

5 Freeman, Josh. *Student Generative AI Survey 2025*. Higher Education Policy Institute and Kortext, February 2025. Accessed December 3, 2025. https://www.hepi.ac.uk/wp-content/uploads/2025/02/HEPI-Kortext-Student-Generative-AI-Survey-2025.pdf.

6 To deep dive into this particular subject, I highly recommend viewing the work of the Emmy-winning nonprofit newsroom, *More Perfect Union*. In particular, these videos are insightful: https://www.youtube.com/watch?v=DGjj7wDYail, https://www.youtube.com/watch?v=YN6BEUA4jNU, and https://www.youtube.com/watch?v=jjkaYyysYhA&t=48s.

7 Doctorow, Cory. *Enshittification: Why Everything Suddenly Got Worse and What to Do About It*. MCD/Farrar, Straus and Giroux, 2025.

8 Paredes, Jose Luis, Smith, Ethan, Druck, Gregory, and Benson, Bevin. "More Articles Are Now Created by AI Than Humans." *Graphite*, 2025. Accessed December 2, 2025. https://graphite.io/five-percent/more-articles-are-now-created-by-ai-than-humans.

9 Mazeika, Mantas, Gatti, Alice, Menghini, Cristina, Sehwag, Udari Madhushani, Singhal, Shivam, Orlovskiy, Yury, Basart, Steven, Sharma, Manasi, Peskoff, Denis, Lau, Elaine, Lim, Jaehyuk, Carroll, Lachlan, Blair, Alice, Sivakumar, Vinaya, Basu, Sumana, Kenstler, Brad, Ma, Yuntao, Michael, Julian, Li, Xiaoke, Ingebretsen, Oliver, Mehta, Aditya, Mottola, Jean, Teichmann, John, Yu, Kevin, Shaik, Zaina, Khoja, Adam, Ren, Richard, Hausenloy, Jason, Phan, Long, Htet, Ye, Aich, Ankit, Rabbani, Tahseen, Shah, Vivswan, Novykov, Andriy, Binder, Felix, Chugunov, Kirill, Ramirez, Luis, Geralnik, Matias, Mesura, Hernán, Lee, Dean, Hernandez Cardona, Ed-Yeremai, Diamond, Annette, Yue, Summer, Wang, Alexandr, Liu, Bing, Hernandez, Ernesto, and Hendrycks, Dan. "Remote Labor Index: Measuring AI Automation of Remote Work." *arXiv*, October 30, 2025. Accessed December 19, 2025. https://doi.org/10.48550/arXiv.2510.2678.

10 White, William. "If Something Cannot Go on Forever, It Will Stop." *Council on Economic Policies*, April 1, 2021. Accessed December 2, 2025. https://www.cepweb.org/if-something-cannot-go-on-forever-it-will-stop/.

11 For a detailed analysis why today's generative AI economics are unsustainable, I highly recommend the work of tech journalist Ed Zitron at https://www.wheresyoured.at/.

12 Zitron, Ed. "There Is No AI Revolution." *Where's Your Ed At*, February 24, 2025. Accessed December 19, 2025. https://www.wheresyoured.at/wheres-the-money/.

13 Sigalos, MacKenzie and Levy, Ari. "Nvidia's Investment in OpenAI Will Be in Cash, and Mostly Will Be Used to Lease Nvidia Chips." *CNBC*, September 24, 2025. Accessed December 19, 2025. https://www.cnbc.com/2025/09/24/nvidia-openai-investment-in-cash-mostly-used-to-lease-nvidia-chips.html.

14 Dweck, Carol S. *Mindset: The New Psychology of Success*. Ballantine Books, 2006.

15 Ibid.

16 For example, see https://doi.org/10.3389/fpsyg.2024.1353271 and https://doi.org/10.55982/openpraxis.16.4.747.

17 Dweck, Carol S. *Mindset: The New Psychology of Success*. Ballantine Books, 2006.

18 Dweck, Carol. "The Power of Believing You Can Improve." *TED*, November 2014. Accessed December 19, 2025. www.ted.com/talks/carol_dweck_the_power_of_believing_that_you_can_improve.

19 To be clear: having a growth mindset isn't willful naiveté, ignoring the potential threats-at-hand, but a potent adaptability trait that is cultivated through choice.

20 Draganski, Bogdan, Gaser, Christian, Busch, Volker, Schuierer, Gerhard, Bogdahn, Ulirch, and May, Arne. "Changes in Grey Matter Induced by Training." *Nature* 427 (2004): 311–312. https://doi.org/10.1038/427311a.

21 Dweck, Carol S. *Mindset: The New Psychology of Success*. Ballantine Books, 2006.

22 Moore, Catherine. "What Is Negativity Bias and How Can It Be Overcome?" *Positive Psychology*, December 30, 2019. Accessed December 19, 2025. https://positivepsychology.com/3-steps-negativity-bias/.

23 Hanson, Rick, Shapiro, Shauna, Hutton-Thamm, Emma, Hagerty, Michael R., and Sullivan, Kevin P. "Learning to Learn from Positive Experiences." *The Journal of Positive Psychology* 18, no. 1 (2023): 142–153. https://doi.org/10.1080/17439760.2021.2006759.

24 Csikszentmihalyi, Mihaly. *Creativity: Flow and the Psychology of Discovery and Invention*. HarperCollins Publishers, 1996.

25 Frankl, Viktor E. *Man's Search for Meaning: An Introduction to Logotherapy*. Beacon Press, 1962.

26 Merriam-Webster. "Purpose." *Merriam-Webster.com Dictionary*. Accessed December 6, 2025. https://www.merriam-webster.com/dictionary/purpose.

27 Oliver, Mary. *New and Selected Poems*. Beacon Press, 1992.

28 Sivers, Derek. *How to Live: 27 Conflicting Answers and One Weird Conclusion*. Hit Media, 2022.

29 de Mille, Agnes. *Martha: The Life and Work of Martha Graham*. Random House, 1991.

30 Buechner, Frederick. *Wishful Thinking: A Theological ABC*. Harper & Row, 1973.

Resources

Further Reading

I'd love to keep the conversation going with you. Please feel free to reach out to me at steven@stevenpotaczek.com if you'd like to connect. I'd also welcome you to visit www.stevenpotaczek.com to keep up on the latest developments since this book was published.

Substacks/Blogs (in alphabetical order):

- Ted Gioia's Substack at https://www.honest-broker.com/.
- Adam Mastroianni's Substack at https://www.experimental-history.com/.
- Brian Merchant's Substack at https://www.bloodinthemachine.com/.
- Ed Zitron's blog at https://www.wheresyoured.at.

Books (in alphabetical order):

- *The Anxious Generation: How the Great Rewiring of Childhood Is Causing an Epidemic of Mental Illness* by Jonathan Haidt.
- *The A.I. Con: How to Fight Big Tech's Hype and Create the Future We Want* by Emily M. Bender and Alex Hanna.
- *Blood in the Machine: The Origins of the Rebellion Against Big Tech* by Brian Merchant.
- *Empire of AI: Dreams and Nightmares in Sam Altman's OpenAI* by Karen Hao.
- *Enshittification: Why Everything Got Worse and What to Do About It* by Cory Doctorow.
- *Ghosts of My Life: Writings on Depression, Hauntology, and Lost Futures* by Mark Fisher.
- *Mood Machine: The Rise of Spotify and the Costs of the Perfect Playlist* by Liz Pelly.
- *On Writing: A Memoir of the Craft* by Stephen King.
- *Real Artists Don't Starve: Timeless Strategies for Thriving in the New Creative Age* by Jeff Goins.

Acknowledgments

I am deeply indebted to many individuals for everything contained within this book.

To Mom, Dad, Philly, Kathryn, and Julie: What a tremendous blessing to have not only been born into a family like ours, but also to be able to "do life" with you. Truly, I love you all more than you know. Mom and Dad, thank you for everything you've given to me, but perhaps most connected to this book, thank you for the gift of music: the lessons, the instruments, the encouragement. To the entire Montanino family: You have always been so supportive; thank you.

To my piano teachers: Gen Yaw (1923–2014) and Mona Tourlentes (1928–2018). Admittedly, these days, I practice piano less than I should, but I create and teach far more than I ever thought I would. Thank you for everything; you set the most perfect example.

To my students and colleagues at Samford University. Each of you inspires me in ways you may never see, but it's true, nonetheless. To my 2025–26 songwriting cohort of Kacie, Eli, Josie, and Eliza: thank you for holding me accountable to write alongside you—keep track of those hours. To Beth McGinnis and Jason Terry: thank you both for encouraging me to write more and showing me the ropes of publishing. You are both such wonderful friends. To Mike Hardin for sitting with me and helping me think about the history of AI. Thank you for being a friend. To Larry Thompson: for fearlessly fighting for the underrepresented and outcast—including me. Now, go practice that guitar. To Joel Davis, Morgan Soja, Theo Metz, and Mark Lackey: you are all such brilliant creatives; I love working with you.

To Philip Peters: thank you for encouraging me to actually release this book. Your support is what gave me the courage to buckle down and make it happen. To Jenaye Merida for the kindness of giving me your time and expertise. I hope we can work together sometime soon! To Erik Anderson for helping me think through the cover design of the book. Thanks for the twenty-five years and counting of being my best friend. To Vince Wilcox, who may be the most loving, giving, and honorable man I know. Thank you for proofing an early chapter and your never-ending support.

Finally, to my girls: Amanda, Stevie, and Bryn. I love you so much, it's hard to think straight. Thank you for letting me be your "Tiki" and "Dad." Those are the greatest titles I could ever wear. I am always here for you. Tap tap tap.

Index

Page numbers in *italics* indicate figures.